MANAGING PEOPLE DURING STRESSFUL TIMES

MANAGING PEOPLE DURING STRESSFUL TIMES

The Psychologically Defensive Workplace

Seth Allcorn
Michael A. Diamond

Q

QUORUM BOOKS
Westport, Connecticut • London

Library of Congress Cataloging-in-Publication Data

Allcorn, Seth.
   Managing people during stressful times : the psychologically
defensive workplace / Seth Allcorn, Michael A. Diamond : foreword by
James Krantz.
     p.   cm.
   Includes bibliographical references and index.
   ISBN 1–56720–082–6 (alk. paper)
   1. Psychology, Industrial.   2. Personnel management—Psychological
aspects.   3. Defensiveness (Psychology)   4. Stress (Psychology)
I. Diamond, Michael A. (Michael Alan), 1950–   .   II. Title
HF5548.8.A646   1997
158.7—dc20   96–17925

British Library Cataloguing in Publication Data is available.

Library of Congress Catalog Card Number: 96–17925
ISBN: 1–56720–082–6

First published in 1997

Quorum Books, 88 Post Road West, Westport, CT 06881
An imprint of Greenwood Publishing Group, Inc.

Printed in the United States of America

The paper used in this book complies with the
Permanent Paper Standard issued by the National
Information Standards Organization (Z39.48–1984).

10 9 8 7 6 5 4 3 2 1

CONTENTS

FIGURES

FOREWORD

The popular management and business press these days is filled with upbeat, optimistic, positive images of the grand future into which we will march, assuming that we link arms and march fearlessly into the unknown with passion, empowerment, creativity, and teamwork under the guidance of transformative leaders. Each nostrum is followed by another; each book holding out the promise of greater glory and success.

Now and then I come across a book that serves as an antidote to the numbing effects of the typical literature. This volume by Seth Allcorn and Michael Diamond provides just this kind of counterpoint. Sober, thoughtful, and grounded, these authors address critical aspects of our emerging organizations clearly without being simplistic. In particular, they examine the psychological impact of today's work settings and confront the very real and troubling reality that is caused by the unceasing turbulence, the ungluing of authority relations, the blinding changes in technology, and the host of other features of our emerging postindustrial world.

Rather than indulging the temptation to proclaim a new future in which problems are transformed into opportunities, the authors address a largely ignored aspect of our situation, namely that today's conditions very often lead to demoralized and disabled workforces, and produce managers who are disoriented and who have lost their bearings.

Depth perspectives concerning human functioning have taught us that under conditions of heightened stress people tend to use less flexible and less sophisticated methods of coping—they "regress." This, in turn, creates what Allcorn and Diamond call the "psychologically defensive workplace," a setting where by virtue of greatly heightened stress, people revert to less sophisticated ways of dealing with work and with colleagues. Competence suffers, morale declines, and performance deteriorates. By "unpacking" these downward spirals, Allcorn and Diamond offer both practitioners and scholars a way of understanding these situations that provides for both deeper appreciation of the forces at play as well as a greater possibility of intervening in the downward spiral. But it is possible to do so only if one faces some of the troubling realities that shape our work settings. The oppressively optimistic and positive popular business press often does just the opposite.

The opportunities for "regression" to defensive postures are great even under "ordinary" conditions, since people must confront the anxiety-laden aspects of performing tasks and must collaborate with supervisors, subordinates, and peers. Many structures, procedures, methods of operating, and organization cultures evolved—in part—to help people contain and manage these anxieties.

Now, however, many of these formerly established features of organizational life are being removed or altered in order to create more responsive, adaptive organizations. While this may make sense from a task perspective, it equally generates many dilemmas, as formerly "contained" anxieties become dislodged. Adding to this are the massive anxieties and doubts arising from the profound uncertainty, change, and insecurity under which so many now work.

Combining an understanding of the diminished capacity for containment with an appreciation for the heightened anxieties leads to a clear recognition of the "regressive" pressures on people and their workplaces in today's world. Allcorn and Diamond address the impact of these pressures at multiple levels of analysis: the individual, the interpersonal realm, the group, the unity, and the whole organization. Similarly, they explore this set of issues from several perspectives: participation and membership, followership, leadership, and consultation.

Altogether, this is an invaluable volume. Rather than leaping to grossly simplistic and idealized images of the future, which I believe exemplify defensive denial of a harsher and more complex reality, Allcorn and Diamond take great care in examining many dimensions of stress and regression in the workplace, and the debilitatingly defensive character of work settings that often emerges as a result. I doubt this will become a best-seller; it is definitely not what anyone wanting a "quick fix" will go for. Nor will it appeal to anyone who simply wants prescriptive answers. The authors provide, however, a kind of theoretically and conceptually rich road map that will be of great assistance to anyone wanting to think carefully about the impact of stress in the workplace or about the presence of defensive patterns of behavior and thought.

As I write this Foreword, I am reminded of so many workplaces where it is considered a minor crime to "be negative," as if expressions of discontent or distress are tantamount to disloyalty and lack of initiative. These settings are, in my view, toxic. In them, learning comes to a standstill, and the irrationality of those in high positions easily comes to dominate the scene in places where others are prohibited from voicing discontent or doubt. As a consultant I have never known how to address this particularly virulent strain of denial: A "dose" of Allcorn and Diamond would be of great use in these organizations.

But all of us—managers, scholars, and consultants alike—desperately need to take our understanding of psychological regression under the impact of workplace stress to deeper levels. Allcorn and Diamond have taken an important step in that direction with this volume.

James Krantz, Ph.D.
Partner, Triad Consulting Group, LLC
Adjunct Associate Professor, Wharton School

PREFACE

The purpose of this book is to draw together our fifteen years of writing, theorizing, and consulting to the workplace. During this time we have tested the efficacy of a psychoanalytically informed approach to understanding human behavior in the workplace. We have learned a lot. In writing this book, we wish to share with executives, human resource managers, consultants, educators, and researchers a comprehensive, systematic, psychologically informed theory of the workplace.

Our book describes an internally consistent and testable theory of how we may understand human behavior in the workplace, in all of its dimensions and complexity. Our goal may be lofty, but not grandiose. We must point out that no new theory is, in fact, being created; rather, existing theories are being extended and elaborated. We, therefore, see this book as building squarely upon, and proceeding from, the work of others. It consolidates and interweaves the work of many authors who have contributed to this growing interest in management and organization theory building.

We have selected five levels of analysis to explore the workplace—intrapersonal, interpersonal, group, organizational, and societal. We believe that comprehensive theories of human behavior in the workplace must have explanatory power for all of these interdependent levels of analysis in order to be comprehensive. We also believe one theoretical perspective must be used to unify the development of a theory of organizational life.

In sum, this book is a challenging theory building project that is informed by many years of research, writing, teaching, and consulting by the authors, and over twenty years of experience as an executive on the part of the first author. The authors have published many parts of the theoretical perspective presented in this book during the past ten years. This book, therefore, is the capstone for this work by pulling it together into a comprehensive theoretical perspective.

ACKNOWLEDGMENTS

We wish to acknowledge those who have provided us nurturance and insights along our path to self and organizational discovery. Many thanks to Guy Adams, Howell Baum, Harry Levinson, Josh Rosenthal, Howard Stein, and our Deans, Bruce Walker and Daniel Winship, who have provided the opportunity and challenge to continue to develop this manuscript. We want to thank Donna Lyle for her good work as our research assistant. We also want to thank our families for their tolerance of the many long hours of solitude required to bring this work to fruition. Last, many thanks to Lt. Savik for her loyal and hovering presence during the preparation of untold revisions and drafts.

INTRODUCTION

The quest goes on in the management literature for a way to master being an effective leader and manager of people in the workplace. The number of books and articles generated on this subject is staggering and continues to grow on a daily basis. No stone seems to have been left unturned in the pursuit of ways to make employees more effective and, therefore, more profitable. Recommended management methods have ranged from the coercive (do it my way or else), through more or less direct and manipulative behavior modification techniques (instant rewards and incentive systems), to more enlightened approaches that tend toward allowing employees ownership of their labor and its products (participative management, total quality management, and quality circles). However, if any of these approaches was the sought-after solution, little more would need to be written. This, however, is not the case: The quest goes on.

One of the reasons (perhaps the primary reason) why effectively managing people remains elusive is the tangle of conscious and unconscious psychological motivations each employee brings to the workplace, to his or her work, and to how he or she relates to others, groups, and the organization. These motivations are unique to each employee and, while they share many things in common, they also possess much personal—often unconscious—content. This unique personal content puts a hard-to-predict personal spin on how people respond to the most well-intended of management methods and actions.

The psychological side of the workplace is falling under ever more scrutiny that is informed by psychoanalytic theory and the work of many authors (Allcorn 1991, 1992, 1994, 1995; Baum 1987; Diamond 1993; Hirschhorn 1988; Kets de Vries 1984, 1991; Kilmann and Kilmann 1994; LaBier 1986; Levinson 1976, 1981; Stein 1994; and Zaleznik 1985). The focus of these authors has been upon various aspects of psychoanalytic theory as it applies to understanding leadership and human behavior in large organizations. Each author made important contributions to developing this new area of intellectual endeavor and research. Many theoretical perspectives have been explored and, when the literature is examined in total, one cannot help but be impressed with the many points of view that arise from trying to understand the impact of psychological defenses upon the workplace. At the same time, these authors have not individually or collectively developed a unified theoretical perspective for understanding the psychologically defensive workplace.

We begin our work with the assumption that all organizations, regardless of whether they are large or small, publicly or privately owned, government enterprises, the military, or a family business, share one thing in common—people. This book is about understanding people in the workplace that they themselves create every day when they come to work. More specifically, it is about the unconscious aspects of their thoughts, feelings, and actions that often underlie the appearance of rationality and control in the workplace.

Organizations and their performance have been extensively examined in theory-building and many other types of research. All of these efforts, however, have thus far shared a common problem: They tend to result in a fragmented approach to understanding people in the workplace. They either place employees in the role of research subjects or, in the case of psychology, employees are studied by using a mix of often incomplete theoretical perspectives and disease classifications.

These approaches, while offering many thoughtful insights, do not, when taken together, offer an overarching internally consistent theoretical understanding of people at work, their relationships with fellow employees, how they work in groups, why and how they design their organizations, and the connection of the workplace to its larger society. As a result, those working, studying, and consulting to people within the workplace must use a mix of management and psychological tools and empirical methods to carry out their work.

Forging a comprehensive, unified, and internally consistent psychoanalytically informed theory of people at work is, however, a difficult task fraught with intellectual tension. The authors have thoroughly explored the workplace implications of one psychodynamic perspective, that of Karen Horney. Her work, as summarized by her 1950 book *Neurosis and Human Growth,* provides researchers a theory of human development and functioning that allows for both personal growth and crippling childhood and interpersonal experiences. Her theoretical perspective introduces a way of understanding unconscious conflict by elaborating the psychological tension between three aspects of human existence: mastery, love, and freedom. It is our contention that her theory possesses the requisite psychoanalytic sophistication to permit insightful theory-building. We also believe that her theory provides a comprehensive, internally consistent way of understanding human behavior in the workplace that enables us to explore all aspects of the workplace and its larger social context.

The authors are, therefore, not attempting to provide yet another theory of human development and behavior; rather, we are expanding the understanding that may be gained by relying upon a "good enough" psychological theory that provides a complete perspective driven by internal conflict. In this regard, ego psychology, object relations theory, and self-psychology are found by the authors to complement Karen Horney's work, which is itself firmly anchored in the interpersonal world.

The development of a comprehensive theoretical perspective permits us to systematically explore the psychologically defensive side of the intrapersonal, interpersonal, group, and organizational aspects of the workplace and its connection to its host society. These aspects of daily work life constitute the levels of analysis we will use to understand our experience of the workplace. Each level of analysis introduces new and ever-greater complexity that builds upon the content of the previous level. The result is a rigorous theoretical intertwining of these levels of analysis to yield an internally consistent theory of the psychologically defensive workplace.

It is also important to mention what this book is—strangely—not about. Organizations contain many things that appear to have concrete and objective existence, such as their chart of organization, written rules and regulations, mottos, mission statements, goals and objectives, financial statements and budgets, physical work areas, and roles that contain power and authority. All of these are aspects of the workplace we are familiar with. As a result, it may seem impossible to describe a theory of the workplace that does not explicitly address these customary artifacts of organizational life. Not doing so would seem to threaten the integrity of any workplace theory.

Our book, however, does not have organizational artifacts of the workplace as its principle focus. They are, nonetheless, frequently discussed as originating in what people think, feel, and do and, in particular, the unconscious side of organizational life that influences thoughts, feelings, and actions. We, therefore, do not take the position that the unconscious side of the workplace is the only important aspect of work, but rather one that coexists with and frequently underlies these more concrete aspects of organizational life.

However, we must also note that in our opinion, these artifacts of the workplace are not, in fact, as concrete and rational as we are often encouraged to believe. We contend that the workplace is filled with many irrationalities that are unacknowledged, difficult to manage, complex, and often ignored. A result of this hard-to-manage complexity is that much effort is expended to find an easy way to motivate and manage people. Regrettably, our position is that an in-depth understanding of human behavior in the workplace reveals that no quick-fix, ten-easy-steps approach to managing people is ultimately going to work.

This book is also not about using psychoanalytic theory as the basis of psychoanalyzing leaders, employees, or the organization. It is neither a clinical text nor a self-help book. It is not intended to provide health-care providers who practice their profession outside of the workplace insights into how to use their clinical skills and knowledge in the workplace. In contrast, this book is about discovering how psychoanalytic theory can be adapted to the study of organizations.

In sum, by providing a comprehensive psychoanalytically informed theory of human behavior in the workplace, we hope to stimulate critical thinking (including criticism of our work); provide empiricists a testable theory; and challenge executives, consultants, teachers, and students of organization to acknowledge the fact that everyone who works has his or her own personal theory of the workplace that may be tested against the comprehensive and integrated theory of human behavior in the workplace presented in this book.

ORGANIZATION OF THE BOOK

Chapter 1 introduces the notion that organizations are social systems that are created by people to, on the surface, organize work. A less-appreciated aspect of formal organization is that it also serves the purpose of providing defenses for individuals, groups, and executives against anxieties that exist in the workplace. It is the nature of these individual, group, and organizational defenses that creates organizational culture and makes organizations different from each other.

Chapter 2 explores the nature of the origins of the assumption of personal responsibility and, in particular, the often appalling lack of willingness on the part of executives to assume personal responsibility for their actions. Executives often resort to psychological defenses to allay their anxieties about the awesome responsibilities they assume leading their organization and its employees. These defenses are found to have many of their roots in early childhood experiences, which become the basis for subsequent coping strategies to fend off stressful aspects of life.

Chapter 3 introduces the concept of psychologically defensive workplace practices, which provide a unifying perspective for understanding the use of psychological defenses in the workplace. A psychological model is described that relates the experience of stress and anxiety and the development of the psychologically defensive workplace practices model (Horney 1950). A response that is not psychologically defensive is provided for comparison.

Chapter 4 introduces the psychologically defensive nature of the interpersonal world at work. Interpersonal relationships are often filled with unpredictability, stress, and anxiety that provoke psychologically defensive interpersonal thoughts, feelings, and actions. Workplace roles are explored for their utilization in the process of enacting psychologically defensive practices.

Chapter 5 examines the psychologically defensive nature of group dynamics in the workplace. The psychologically defensive practices are recast in the form of three psychologically defensive appeals: the appeals to mastery, love, and freedom. These appeals provide a conceptual window for understanding the unconscious and psychologically defensive nature of group dynamics. In particular, groups that develop a consistent reliance upon specific psychologically defensive group dynamics may be understood to have developed a psychologically defensive group culture.

Chapter 6 expands upon the notion of group culture by describing the psychologically defensive nature of organizations and their cultures. The nature of organizational culture is described and analyzed for its contribution to defending organizational members and executives from anxiety. The three psychologically defensive appeals (mastery, love, and freedom) are redescribed as the basis for three psychologically defensive organizational cultures or organizational identities: autocratic, institutional, and homogenized. Leader and follower relationships are discussed from the point of view that psychologically defensive motivations are enacted by the psychological defenses splitting, projection, and projective identification.

Chapter 7 concludes the analysis of psychologically defensive elements of the workplace by examining the contribution psychologically defensive practices make to the shaping of the larger society in which organizations exist. The influences social values and norms have upon the shaping of organizations and the psychologically defensive tendencies that executives and employees bring with them into the workplace are also discussed.

Chapter 8 presents an analysis of leadership styles and suggestions to improve leadership that are anchored in the psychologically defensive tendencies that exist within organizations. Psychologically defensive leadership styles are described and case examples are provided. The nature of psychologically defensive organizational change is also examined, as is the need for developing nondefensive leadership styles.

Chapter 9 describes the implications of the psychologically defensive workplace for organizational and management consulting. The importance of making a carefully developed organizational diagnosis is explained. The vast array of findings that are uncovered during the diagnostic phase are made sense of by organizing them around the theoretical perspectives of this book, which also inform the development of organizational intervention strategies.

Chapter 10 concludes the book by providing readers with suggestions as to how to better manage and participate in the psychologically defensive workplace. Consideration is also given to life beyond the workplace. The psychological model also provides a basis for appreciating the complexities of daily life.

We hope that you find this book of value in your work and, perhaps more important, thought provoking.

THE PSYCHOLOGICALLY DEFENSIVE WORKPLACE $\quad$ 1

> The actual working of institutions takes place through real people using cultural mechanisms within a social structure; and the unconscious, or implicit functions of an institution are specifically determined by the particular individuals associated in the institution, occupying roles within a structure and operating the culture.
>
> $\qquad$ Jaques 1955, 279

> The characteristic feature of the social defense system, as we have described it, is its orientation toward helping the individual avoid the experience of anxiety, guilt, doubt and uncertainty.
>
> $\qquad$ Menzies 1960, 415

Organizations are social systems created by people. Their presumably impersonal and rational designs are most often thought of as organizing people and work. However, a less-appreciated aspect of organizational life is that it is also filled with individual, interpersonal, group, and organizational defenses against the inevitable anxieties that exist in the workplace. Organization theorists claim that in addition to traditional social, economic, political, and cultural uses of organizations, people use psychological defenses and workplace social systems to defend themselves against anxiety (Diamond 1993). In fact, Jaques (1955) and Menzies (1960) argue that organization members are often held together by psychologically defensive practices that contribute to the creation of anxiety controlling workplace social systems. How organizations operate and what distinguishes them one from another may, therefore, be understood to depend, in part, upon the nature of individual and shared psychological defenses that are enacted to create the psychologically defensive workplace (Allcorn 1994; Diamond 1993). The psychologically defensive workplace not only encourages the use of individual and interpersonal psychological defenses, it encourages individual, group, and organizational reliance upon common organizational artifacts such as hierarchy, specialization, and roles, to further control workplace anxiety. The persistence of hierarchical, rule-bound bureaucratic organizations can, therefore, be understood to be an outcome of not only organizing work but also the psychologically defensive workplace.

BUREAUCRACY: AN ENDURING WAY OF ORGANIZATIONAL LIFE

Despite the influence of nearly thirty years of organization development and management fads, the bureaucratic organization form is alive and well. Most contemporary complex organizations continue to fit Max Weber's (1947) description of bureaucracy: (1) a hierarchy of authority relationships, (2) administrative rules to guide organizational tasks, (3) decision making according to technical and legal rules, (4) the maintenance of files and records, enhanced today by computer technology and management information systems, and (5) the notion of administration as a vocation in which the private lives of those who run organizations are considered to be separate from the position occupied. These attributes encourage organizational norms and rigidity that account for worker alienation and the slow responsiveness to change that is so deeply ingrained in contemporary organizations.

Bureaucratic organization and work design deter people from sharing thoughts, feelings, and ideas. Hierarchical workplace relationships and vertically oriented and controlled information flows inhibit, distort, and fragment communication between people and across organizational boundaries. Bureaucratic hierarchy, functional specialization, detailed division of labor and professionalization have split people apart, thereby promoting interpersonal anxiety and making self-protective psychological defenses not only acceptable but often the norm. As a result, a fortress-like mentality often develops over administrative jurisdictions that produces paranoid turf battles among members of organizational units, divisions, and departments. Managers learn to resist delegating authority and decision making, and do not learn to share information or permit joint possession of tasks. Not surprisingly, subordinates do not learn to collaborate. Rather than developing cooperative systems, as Chester Barnard (1948) would have it, bureaucracy promotes competitive, self-protective, risk aversive, and discordant workplace social systems.

Executives have tried to counter these problems of bureaucracy by flattening hierarchies; adapting participative management philosophies; and experimenting with "quality circles," "team-building," and, most recently, total quality management (TQM) and reengineering techniques; but to no avail. Organization participants still feel alienated and anxious (frequently because of these methods) and question the sincerity of their superiors (Allcorn, Baum, Diamond, and Stein 1996). When one worker in a large organization was asked how he felt about the participative management philosophy hanging on the wall of his office, he remarked, "Oh that, everyone around here knows it's a joke!" The worker understood that although top management claimed to support a collaborative and participative philosophy, there were few occasions when these principles were actually practiced. In other words, as Argyris and Schon (1974, 1978) have noted, upper management often says one thing and does another. They (upper management) are not to be taken seriously or trusted. On the surface, staff may poke fun at the contradictions but, in fact, they feel angry, resentful, and manipulated by upper management's deceptions. Disappointed and guilt-ridden over their hostile emotions, staff end up suppressing and otherwise psychologically defending themselves against these distressing, dangerous, and anxiety-ridden feelings in order to adapt to a bureaucratic culture that denies them authentic participation and the freedom and safety to express their feelings and ideas.

In sum, Max Weber's system of rationally organized human action may, in practice, be understood to include a self-perpetuating, socially defensive system that promotes employee psychological defensiveness and counterproductive and uncooperative workplace activities. The values of high control versus service, technical rationality versus reflectivity, self-protection versus trust, and the suppression of negative feelings versus openness often creates an unrelentingly hostile and anxiety-filled work environment (Argyris and Schon 1978; Baum 1987; Crozier 1964; Hummel 1977; Kraus 1980; Schon 1983). Bureaucratic organization, which minimizes anxiety by maximizing interpersonal defensiveness and maintaining the status quo, may, therefore, be understood to be both cause and effect (Argyris and Schon 1974, 1978; Diamond 1984, 1985; Diamond and Allcorn 1985; Jaques 1955; Menzies 1970). Understanding this unacknowledged hidden agenda of controlling thoughts, feelings, and behavior, which, in turn, promotes alienation and anxiety and consequently the need for more control, necessitates developing an appreciation of the subjective experience of work life. If we wish to understand the workplace so that we might change it, we must comprehend its psychosocial origins.

THE PSYCHOSOCIAL ORIGINS OF BUREAUCRACY

In part, people create bureaucratic organizations to fulfill their deepest needs for interpersonal control and security. Executives and employees enjoy predictable work environments. They readily master techniques for accomplishing tasks and controlling each other. They intuitively understand that routinizing human relations at work limits interpersonal anxieties by making the behavior of others, operations, and interactions with the public or marketplace predictable.

The degree to which workers use psychological defenses and bureaucratic rules, regulations, and hierarchy as a defense against workplace anxiety depends upon the degree to which stressful conditions are present and the workers' levels of self-esteem. If employees feel anxious and threatened by workplace events, and are therefore more psychologically defensive, they are less willing to assume personal responsibility, which is crucial to any strategy for reducing workplace anxiety and transcending bureaucracy and the psychologically defensive workplace.

In order to appreciate that modern-day bureaucratic organizations are, in part, a psychologically defensive system that defends employees against workplace anxieties, the origin of psychological defenses in the development of a sense of self must be explained.

ATTACHMENT, SEPARATION, AND THE SELF

Life begins in an attached state. Mother and child are merged. Infant research indicates that some degree of cognitive differentiation between self and other exists for infants at birth, so that the self may be described as emergent (Stern 1985), rather than dedifferentiated or autistic (Mahler, Pine, and Bergman 1975). Nonetheless, the emergent self is dependent upon the parent's ability to love and nurture it—what psychoanalysts of the object-relations school term the "holding environment" and Otto Kernberg (1980) calls "object constancy" (Bowlby 1969; Fairbairn 1952; Winnicott 1965; Guntrip 1969). Both concepts refer to the infant's developmental requirement for accessible, stable, predictable, and relatively anxiety-free nurturing from parents. Parents must be able to place their children's needs before their own. They must successfully interpret the meaning of their baby's signals for contact, comfort, and tenderness, and they must be capable of positively responding to the infant's narcissistic desire for grandiosity, for omnipotence, and to idealize his or her parents (Kohut 1977). However, when infants do not receive adequate nurturing, they experience the interpersonal world as one filled with uncertainty and paranoid feelings of basic anxiety (Horney 1950). In sum, self-development occurs from birth through adulthood along a continuum from dependence to independence, provided that the child receives good enough parenting (Fairbairn 1952; Winnicott 1965).

However, good enough parenting is not always the case. When parental attachment is insecure, infantile feelings of engulfment or abandonment characterize the baby's experience. Engulfment signifies a child's fear of infanticide (Bloch, 1978), or feeling smothered out of existence by too much attention and too many controlling expectations. In contrast, abandonment represents fantasized or actual loss of attachment and, by extension, affection and approval and even the basic necessities to sustain life (Bowlby 1980). Bowlby (1969), for instance, describes the behavior of the attached child as clinging and following. This behavior is normal among infants at the early stages of individuation.

However, excessive clinging and following to avoid abandonment may continue into later childhood and, therefore, restrict the child's willingness to explore and experiment in the absence of the mother or father.

In sum, when parental attachment is experienced as overwhelming, insecure, unavailable, and unsafe, the development of basic anxiety thwarts the child's ability to individuate and become a separate, whole person with defensible self/ other boundaries (Bowlby 1973; Horney 1950). The degree to which basic anxiety is experienced by the child also determines his or her reliance upon life-draining psychological defenses throughout life (Allcorn 1992).

Childhood attachment anxieties are retained as unconscious memories which, under stressful circumstances, reemerge in the workplace along with associated psychological defenses that the child learned helped him or her to cope with the anxieties. It is not uncommon to find adults in the workplace fighting off engulfment and crying out for attachment. Employees often want to be left alone or to be taken care of. Furthermore, they often seek these outcomes with minimal provocation and without question, which is often indicative of unresolved childhood attachment issues.

The distressing experience of attachment anxiety leads the infant, child, and adult to learn to cope with their out-of-control, threatening life experience by using a mix of reliable, familiar, and, therefore, unquestioned psychological defenses in the workplace. There are a number of common psychological defenses against anxiety that are relied upon, individually and in combination, to combat excessive attachment anxiety. Understanding how these defenses are interwoven to create consistent and identifiable patterns of behavior (character) creates an underlying framework for understanding the psychologically defensive workplace.

PSYCHOLOGICAL DEFENSES AGAINST WORKPLACE ANXIETY

There are many psychological defenses that people engage in at work and elsewhere. The psychological defenses discussed here form the basis of readily observable, interpersonally defensive workplace behavior which, when adopted by others, creates the psychologically defensive workplace.

Repression

The concept of repression is the foundation of theories of unconscious process. Freud puts it simply: "The essence of repression lies simply in turning something away, and keeping it at a distance, from the conscious" (1989). Repression is the most powerful psychological defense against anxiety associated with a dangerous situation. The need for repression arises when social taboos conflict with gratifying forbidden pleasures, thereby provoking anxiety within the individual. A child may be in a murderous rage to be rid of its mother. Awareness of the desire (or hidden pleasure) and fear of her loss and accompanying self-annihilation is diminished by shutting the impulse out of awareness behind a barrier of repression. The desire becomes unconscious through a process of resisting all thoughts, images, and actions related to the rage and desire: They vanish. Recovery of the repressed content requires the working through of the resistance in psychoanalysis. The psychoanalytic setting provides a safe holding environment to permit the weakening of defensive ego functions and self-protective and -deceptive thoughts, feelings, and actions. In technical terms, the desire is recovered through the "return of the repressed" and "lifting of the repression barrier." In the case of organizations, similar resistance to dealing with anxiety-provoking aspects of the workplace must be diminished in much the same way to encourage the development of insight and the emergence of problem-solving skills.

Leadership transitions, layoffs, restructuring and redesign, rapid expansions, technological innovations, unresolved conflicts, major problems, and the like are threatening organizational events that weaken defensive ego functions among employees. In the face of these kinds of change, normal, everyday adaptive behaviors often become ineffective and dysfunctional. As feelings of chaos emerge, collective anxieties frequently increase as organizational members perceive the situation as ever more threatening. If they come to feel too anxious, they may unwittingly collude to collectively repress anxiety-producing knowledge of change, interpersonal conflicts, administrative inconsistencies and contradictions, errors and deficiencies, and their disappointed expectations—all of which signal a distressing loss of control. In other words, they may deny or disavow their experience of an incident and act as if the event did not occur or will be magically resolved without effort on their part. It is worth noting that external intervention and analysis of the unconscious life of an organization is potentially the most useful to organizational leaders and members at this point.

A vice president becomes anxious when he is caught in a leadership transition that replaces his previous "hands-off" CEO with a proactive, "hands-on" micromanaging change agent (Diamond and Allcorn 1986). The vice president first acknowledges and then denies the loss of control over his work and continues to function as if he were in charge of his work as in the past. The result is that he avoids dealing with his anger and rage by avoiding confronting his depressive feelings associated with disappointment over the change in his role and authority. In addition uncertainty as to who is in charge leads to lower staff morale, and operations deteriorate. The deeply personal nature of this response to change is often best addressed by external consultation.

Regression

Regression is a metaphorical return to earlier modes of human relations where stage-appropriate conflicts reemerge in the present. To put it simply, adults act child-like, not in a playful way but rather in a manner that expresses conflict and the holding of unrealistic expectations for others. A man in bed with the flu, for example, may become excessively needy and demanding of his wife. He feels the need to play up the seriousness of his illness and continually catalogue the severity and number of his symptoms. He expects his wife to be a constant sympathetic presence at his bedside—in other words, to treat him in a manner that compensates for attachment anxiety associated with neglect on the part of his mother (transference is discussed later) when he was sick as a child. In sum, illness on the man's part triggers feelings of abandonment that belong to experiences with his mother and place excessive demands on his wife.

Psychological regression, many psychoanalysts believe, serves the purpose of protecting individuals from the perceived threat of psychological death of the self. Regression permits the individual to fantasize his or her withdrawal into a safe and secure inner space—a womblike space of total dependency and lack of adult responsibilities. As an unconscious fantasy, it offers a metaphorical return to the earliest relationship between mother and infant, that which Winnicott (1965) calls the holding environment. It represents that space in time before separation and individuation—the attached state of complete dependency on someone else.

Regressive behavior is also provoked among organizational members in response to anxiety-ridden workplace events. For example, an announcement of a downsizing may be experienced by organization members as abandonment that takes the form of withdrawal of organizational commitment and support by top management (loss of the good parent). Employees come to feel unjustly treated and, consequently, regress to a childlike mental state of totalistic bifurcated thinking, where people and objects are categorized (split) into all-or-nothing terms. Everything seems white or black; good or bad. Employees feel like helpless victims and come to perceive themselves as "all good," and others (another section, department, division, or top management) as victimizers and "all bad." Distressing removal of organizational support triggers an escape among organization members into an alternate reality. Their regression is facilitated by other psychological defenses, such as splitting and projection.

Splitting

Splitting is an essential component of projection and projective identification (discussed in the next section). It involves the separation of the self (or others as objects in one's mind) into two parts. The tendency to perceive self and others as either ideal (all good) or despicable (all bad) is the consequence of splitting. Splitting also arouses emotions attached to good and bad experience, which can vastly accentuate the need to defend against one or the other of the images (Kernberg 1980). As in life, splitting occurs in organizations under stressful conditions. Staff, who under normal conditions are whole (with both good and bad qualities), split their self-images and images of others into idealized and despised perceptions of self and others. Someone who fears a colleague's rejection may feel worthless and despised. The individual separates good, worthwhile self feelings, from bad, worthless self feelings thereby setting the stage for getting rid of one of the conflicting attitudes to minimize internal conflict and anxiety. In this case, good self experience is split off, denied, and projected (possibly onto the other individual, who becomes an all-good image) to fulfill an unconscious need to feel unworthy of acceptance (i.e., the person actually deserves to be rejected). It is equally possible to have the bad, worthless self experience projected, leaving the individual feeling that he or she is good and worthy of being accepted and that it is the other, rejecting person who is bad.

Projection

Projection gets rid of the split-off, unwanted anxiety-promoting part of self or other experience (Laplanche and Pontalis 1973). It is a mental process that places the "bad" or "good" part of self within an internal image of someone, in an effort to take control of him or her (projective identification). Projection, as noted, commences with splitting experience into good and bad and the denial of one of these aspects of self or others, thereby creating good (accepting) or bad (rejecting) images. Anxiety about holding both of these conflicting experiences simultaneously is then minimized by expelling one set of feelings and holding onto the opposing feelings. These internal manipulations of thoughts and feelings relative to mental images of others often leaks out to influence the interpersonal world. "One denies that one feels such and such an emotion, has such and such a wish, but asserts that someone else does" (Rycroft 1968). When the splitting and projective process is externalized, it forms the basis of projective identification (discussed in the next section), which is an effort to control the person who is the focal point of the projected content.

Executives are subjected to projection of both good and bad images. Subordinates may project their good parts onto their images of their superiors, while retaining their bad parts where these projections begin to influence interpersonal relations. Executives who take in (identify with, introject) these projected idealized self-images often come to feel expansive and act narcissistically, while their subordinates, who retain despised self-images, feel worthless and self-effacing and act dependently. Executives may inadvertently reinforce this unconscious interpersonal dynamic by splitting off and projecting their worthless and negative feelings onto their staff, thereby reinforcing the staff's negative self-images and their idealized images of themselves. It is also possible that the staff may be unable to contain their bad feelings about themselves. This can result in a search to identify someone else to project their bad experience onto. Identification of an external enemy or scapegoat is often the preferred destination. The scapegoat, instead of part of oneself, may then be hated and disposed of.

Jaques (1955) discusses a first officer on a ship who the crew feels is responsible for many things that go wrong even though he is not actually responsible. He is, in effect, blamed (scapegoated) by the crew for their bad experiences. According to Jaques, the crew's bad objects and impulses are unconsciously put into the first officer. He is then regarded by common consent as the source of the crew's problems and can be openly hated. As a result, the crew finds relief from their own internal conflict and persecutors by displacing their aggression held for themselves and others (in particular the captain, who is responsible) onto the first officer. This permits the ship's captain to be more readily idealized and identified as a highly effective and protective figure (something that is critically important during war time). For Jaques, projection is a way to deflect bad feelings, often associated with anger and hostility, onto someone else to permit maintaining idealized self-images or, in the case of the captain, an idealized image of someone else. In sum, scapegoating the first officer permits the crew to deny their individual and collective responsibility for their feelings, which serves to sustain their idealized self-images and attachment to their idealized captain.

Projective Identification

Projective identification is a mode of projection in which the subject locates part of him- or herself in someone else which permits knowing this person to have the projected attributes (Klein, 1946). At the same time, the other takes in or introjects (discussed later) the projected content to become like the projection. Controlling others (into which parts of the self are projected) is central to projective identification. Anna Freud's notion of "living through another person"—what she calls "altruistic surrender"—exemplifies this process (Sandler 1987). The object's acceptance of the projection distinguishes the act of projective identification from ordinary projection. Projective identification, therefore, differs from projection in that the one who projects part of him- or herself into the other, is able to experience that split-off part through the other. The object of projection must accept the subject's projected image, thereby allowing him- or herself to be controlled as an object by the subject.

Thomas Ogden explains,

In projective identification, the projector induces a feeling state in another that corresponds to a state that the projector had been unable to experience himself. The object is enlisted in playing a role in an externalized version of the projector's unconscious psychological state. When a recipient of a projective identification allows the induced state to reside within him without immediately attempting to rid himself of these feelings, the projector–recipient pair can experience that which had been projected in a manner unavailable to the projector alone. (1990, 35)

Projective identification is revealed in fantasies in which the subject inserts him- or herself, in whole or in part, into the other in order to harm, possess, or control him or her (Laplanche and Pontalis 1973). It is, therefore, a form of unconscious manipulation, such as that which occurs between subordinates and executives in the workplace, and between groups of people and individuals. Freud (1921) claims, for example, that leaders who are idealized (through projection) come to experience themselves as ideal by taking in idealizing projections as projective identification. This idealized image of the leader is then introjected by followers and becomes a substitute for their individual ego ideals. This two-way process of projective identification and introjection unconsciously joins leaders and followers together, thereby enabling the group or organization to function under the authority of the leader. Although Freud did not refer to it as such, the introjection of the projection is an example of what Melanie Klein (1948) calls "projective identification." Unconscious processes such as these are common occurrences in the workplace.

The members of a committee feel great frustration with their designated chairwoman who, they think, is dragging her feet and avoiding making important decisions. Consequently, members look for an ideal person to replace her. A male colleague is selected. They communicate to him their loss of patience and helplessness and their wish for him to do something to help move the process along (rescue them). As a result, he begins to feel their intense frustration and helplessness, but is also idealized, which leads him to feel that he must act to save them, thereby inadvertently validating their experience of themselves as ineffective, helpless, and dependent. The process of projective identification is complete. He takes a more proactive, idealized risk-taking stance during the next meeting by intervening in the group's process often enough to get the chairwoman to reluctantly move ahead.

Introjection

Introjection is the opposite of projection. It entails the "taking in" of the external world. Our internal and external worlds are differentiated by boundaries between self (subject) and other (object). Introjection involves the taking of the experience of another person into the self thereby making this experience part of the self. Introjection serves several purposes and may occur in several forms as a defense against anxiety.

Internalization of the experience of parents and significant others into the child's fantasy world may provide the child with inherent security by the reassuring (introjected) presence of the other (Sandler 1987). Introjection of a loving, nurturing, "good mother" reinforces object constancy in the child, which is a prerequisite to individuation, self-esteem, and interpersonal security. The child constructs a sense of his or her own ideals and conscience by identifying with introjections of parents and other significant people. Conversely, introjection of unpredictable, judgmental, critical, and punitive parental figures provides the child with a paucity of constant and soothing self-regulatory internal objects and the child comes to know him- or herself as unable to control him- or herself and not worthy of proper caretaking.

The notion of identification with the introject is helpful in understanding the workplace. For example, socializing new employees involves their assuming or taking as part of themselves institutional values and norms. If successful, it can be said that members introject the superego and ego ideal of the executives, or the organization ego ideal (Schwartz 1990), by taking these idealized images (as objects for identification) into themselves and then identifying with these internal others.

Similarly, the character of the leader's introjected childhood images affect the manner in which he or she executes roles of authority in the organization, and the manner in which he or she uses or abuses power. Introjection of an abusive and punitive parent can result in identification with the aggressor and the assumption of an intimidating and authoritarian management style.

Compromise and Reaction Formations

For Freud, neurotic symptoms are manifestations of compromise formations, which are products of conflict that signify both sides to the conflict (Klein 1976). A balance or compromise is unconsciously created between two competing impulses. The result of the compromise is that neither side is dealt with or acted upon and the conflict is sustained unconsciously, thereby creating compulsive reliance upon the compromise to suppress both impulses.

Laplanche and Pontalis (1973) describe compromise-formation as a form of repressed memory that later returns in symptoms and dreams and, more generally, in all products of the unconscious. The repressed memory is distorted by defenses against it, to the point of being unrecognizable. Murderous contempt and hate-filled childhood impulses arising from narcissistic injuries may be so threatening and unacceptable to the child's well-being (the opposing impulse) that they are forgotten (unconsciously repressed). The compromise works because it secures attachment without the experience of internal conflict with bad images of self and the needed other. The bad images cease to exist, thereby frequently permitting other, often opposite feelings to emerge, such as love and approval. These opposite feelings constitute a reaction formation which further enables the individual to master the unacceptable impulses and feelings by continually focusing awareness on doing just the opposite. However, as noted, the unacceptable impulses and opposing feelings continue to exist, which necessitates compulsive reliance upon the psychological defenses of the compromise formation and the reaction formation to keep them under control. The person's psychologically defensive nature and compulsive thoughts, feelings, and actions cannot be questioned without threatening the emergence of the internal conflict and accompanying anxiety and loss of self-integration. The result is personal rigidity, inflexibility, and an overwhelming need to stay in control of interpersonal relationships to control one's anxieties.

Joining and participating in organizations also involves adjustment. The new employee must strike a compromise between the unconscious requirements of his or her personality and the demands of the organization. These compromises are worked out in organizational role formations, where the employee reshapes his or her assigned role to more closely fit his or her unconscious demands. In fact, the defensive practices described in Chapter 3 are compromise and reaction formations. They represent the individual's unconscious resolution of conflicting demands in action, what Horney (1950) calls "neurotic solutions."

Yet another aspect of psychological life that, while not a psychological defense to anxiety, influences the perception of work life as secure or unsafe and desirable or aversive, is the effect that prior life experience has upon understanding and responding to the context of the moment. This aspect of daily life is transference.

TRANSFERENCE: THE BASIS FOR SHARED
EMOTIONS AND RELATIONAL PATTERNS AT WORK

The workplace is filled with many feelings unrelated to the workplace and events of the moment. Many of these emotions are less than visibly shared and, therefore, can become a confusing and anxiety-ridden part of the workplace. People come to know each other for who they are, but also, in part, for who they resemble from prior life experience. People usually unwittingly attribute much to others they hardly know and with whom they have had little experience. As a result, people often react to others on the grounds of untested assumptions, imagination, and fantasy. The notion of transference explains this process.

Transference is the basis for unconscious sharing of similar emotions among employees, in which feelings and attitudes attached to one or more past relationships (to mother, father, siblings, former spouses, or workplace experiences) are unconsciously attached to an individual, group, or situation in the present. This creates near-perfect certainty (pathological certainty, often enhanced by projection) that the person is like the person in the past (in particular, possessing the same interpersonal motivations), which blocks the ability to know the person for who he or she really is (Diamond 1993).

A new supervisor may physically resemble a much-detested superior from the distant past. Consequently, employees may well feel that they know their supervisor's modus operandi (critical, punishing, self-centered and self-promoting motivations) and hold their new boss in contempt before they get to know his or her values, management style, and temperament. This process may well lead to employee splitting, projection, and projective identification to fulfill these unconscious expectations and fantasies.

Employees invariably hold unconscious expectations for their boss. These expectations often originate from individually and collectively frustrated needs for idealization and merger with greatness, strength, and calmness stemming from childhood or prior work experience. The disappointment remains repressed until a new relationship unconsciously renews the repressed desire. Employees may want to feel that their boss is superhuman and perfect and, therefore, begin to treat him or her as infallible (projective identification) to fulfill their need for merger with an omnipotent authority figure who can be idealized. At the same time, the executive's unconscious need for aggrandizement and adoration may be triggered by anxieties about past problems associated with assuming personal responsibility, and by the interpersonal pressure of his or her idealizing employees to take charge. The executive begins to feel highly effective and valued as a reaction to his or her feelings of inadequacy and fear, and as an unconscious emotional reaction to his or her employees feeling that he or she is omnipotent. In this example, feelings of inadequacy originate from within the executive (self-doubt) and lead to the opposite feelings of being highly effective (a reaction formation). At the same time, the executive feels special and liked in the eyes of his or her idealizing employees and obliged to act heroically to fulfill their expectations of being taken care of (dependency).

In sum, transference originates from within as a response to the feelings and actions of others and may be contrasted to projective identification, where projected content of others is intended to take over control from the executive via introjection. The executive is to act heroically or risk disapproval. Transference, therefore, further blurs self and other boundaries between the executive and employees. Unconscious fantasy, conflict, ambivalence, and ambiguity come to dominate work life.

Workplace anxiety, psychological defensiveness, and the effects of prior life experience upon experience of the moment create a complex, ever-shifting subjective experience of the interpersonal world that is more or less grounded in objective reality. What must be appreciated is that this phantom world of psychological defenses and subjectivity can either encourage or discourage the assumption of personal responsibility for one's own thoughts, feelings, and actions, as will be discussed in Chapter 2.

SUMMARY

The origins of the psychologically defensive workplace arise from the need to defend against workplace anxiety. The psychological defensiveness is externalized in the form of the need to control others, work, and events. These defenses are often operationalized in the form of hierarchical, rule-bound, bureaucratic organizations, where roles and work are carefully defined and coordinated, and where power, which is exercised from the top down, is also routinized to make it relatively more safe and predictable for those against whom it may be used. Hierarchical organizations that meet the criteria of bureaucracy are, therefore, understood to contain elements of (if not substantially based upon) the need to develop a socially defensive system of interpersonal and role relationships to avoid anxiety.

THE PSYCHOLOGICAL ORIGINS OF PERSONAL RESPONSIBILITY

2

These professionals are well paid and highly regarded, and they have various amounts of influence. But money, status, and power are not enough. They want work organizations to allow them to be competent, to affiliate with colleagues in specific ways, to see results of their efforts, and, above all, to maintain their self-esteem.

Baum 1990, 29

The main focus of the adult in his work and career is to establish awareness of himself as a unique individual while contributing to his society. The complete merger of his identity within any social structure results in a gradual loss of feeling and responsibility. This loss reverberates throughout the entire life performance of the individual at work, in the family, and the community.

Zaleznik 1966, 23

The psychologically defensive workplace has, as its underlying foundation, avoiding anxiety on the part of executives and employees associated with losses of control of fellow employees, one's work, customers, and clients. Bureaucratic systems of rules, regulations, roles, protocols, and top-down, one-way communication are common ways that sought-after control is acquired. Organizational failure is, therefore, often viewed to be the product of imperfect control on the part of management who, in turn, blame others (employees, customers, clients, competitors, government) who are, it is claimed, resistant to control and imperfectly compliant (possibly leading to reorganization and downsizing, thereby eliminating the "bad" employees who are the problem). It is also understood that the extent to which these types of control are felt to be necessary is influenced by the degree to which executives and employees possess and maintain adequate self-esteem. Adequate self-esteem permits them to feel comfortable with others and work and avoid feeling anxious, even though the workplace is, at times, filled with stressful experience and occasionally the chaotic thoughts, feelings, and actions of others.

The psychologically defensive, control-oriented, bureaucratic workplace leads to well-documented problems, such as rigidity, lack of adaptiveness, and the alienation of employees, customers, and clients (Downs 1967; Jacoby 1973). It also leads to an often dramatic avoidance of the assumption of personal responsibility for one's thoughts, feelings, and actions, as well as those of others (Diamond and Allcorn 1984).

When control (or, more likely, the lack thereof) becomes an issue, events are associated with "them" or "it" and, seemingly more often these days, "the consultants," who accomplish change by the numbers. Executives who are personally responsible for what happens are seldom named other than to be scapegoated. The sense of danger that accompanies losses of control often leads to the mentality of merely doing what one is told to do without question (to keep one's job). In the event that what is done adversely affects others, the explanation is, "I (or we) were just following orders (or the rules and regulations)." The ability to think or say, "Just a minute, this isn't right," is lost in the pursuit of safety and security symbolically wrapped in bureaucratic red tape, protocol, and job security. Horrific problems and events that occur (such as downsizing) seem to be no one's responsibility.

It is, therefore, critical to explore the relationship between psychological defensiveness and personal responsibility in order to be able to find ways to improve individual, group, and organizational effectiveness during stressful times. Personal responsibility and irresponsibility may be examined by using Winnicott's (1965) notion of true and false self and Kohut's (1977) views on narcissism. It must also be noted that Winnicott's notion of the false self is similar to Deutsch's (1942) original concept of the "as if personality," and Sullivan's (1953) "as if performer."

PERSONAL RESPONSIBILITY

The origins of personal responsibility lie in the earliest relationship between parent and child. Individual responses to stressful circumstances in organizations ultimately depend upon the degree to which the infant and child experience relationships with caretaking others as safe, secure, and promoting personal autonomy and self-worth. The potential for the child to act with intentionality, willfulness, and self-agency may end up being repressed during infancy and childhood as a response to parents who, consumed by their own needs, are unable to sensitively respond to their child's need for love and affection, recognition, and approval.

Narcissistic, depressed, and otherwise psychologically distressed parents have difficulty seeing beyond themselves and their many personal needs. As a result, they require their babies and children to satisfy their many frustrated needs for admiration and idealization (Kohut 1977). These parents, who possess low self-esteem (or what Kohut calls self-deficits), do not, therefore, respond adequately to their child's original and healthy narcissism. The child's developmental requirements for loving and adoring, mirroring, and idealization are not met. Rather, the parents become anxious and controlling as their children show evidence of separation, individuation, and autonomous behavior (Mahler, Pine, and Bergman 1975).

These anxious and self-centered parents respond by discouraging self-fulfilling autonomous moves on the part of their children and encouraging them to be as the parent desires. These parents manipulate the amount and quality of love and affection they provide their children, thereby frustrating their children's developing sense of autonomy. These parents may also become frustrated and anxious about a child's natural behavior, such as crying, eating, vomiting, and waste elimination. The child, sensing the parent's anxiety and frustration, comes to feel anxious about him- or herself, habits, and bodily functions, thereby further encouraging change away from self-acceptable and normal self-functioning.

In the absence of "good enough mothering," Winnicott (1965) claims, the false self emerges to protect and keep under wraps the painful existence of a rejected and dominated true self. The spontaneous true self becomes split off and repressed and is replaced by a predominantly compliant false self that forms a protective screen against self-annihilating anxiety perpetuated by parents and others (Masterson 1988). The child learns to act in ways expected by others and, consequently, the seeds of personal autonomy and responsibility do not sprout and the child develops a self-deficit (like his or her parents). In this way, a vicious cycle is set in motion that is passed from one generation to the next.

Although a psychological defense, the false self and accompanying deficit, it must be acknowledged, are adaptive behavior that cope with an uncertain and sometimes hostile interpersonal world. The child attempts to control others by controlling his or her thoughts, feelings, and actions (to be as others desire) in order to secure loving attachment and some degree of personal autonomy. The child willingly changes him- or herself in what amounts to a self-imposed process of seeking control over others through controlling oneself. This ultimately self-defeating interpersonal strategy ironically leads to the feared threat of self-annihilation (through repression of the true self) and, as an adult, the compulsive pursuit of interpersonal control is often acted out in the form of the codependent personality (Allcorn 1992).

In sum, for Winnicott (1965), all of us have multiple personalities that are comprised of false self-organizations that defend us against the anxiety of engulfment and abandonment. The false self is triggered by anxiety brought on by relationships among family members, lovers, friends, and fellow workers and stressful workplace events. However, the presence of the false self in the workplace encourages conformity, mediocrity, and authoritarianism among workers and an emphasis upon control via psychological defensiveness and bureaucratization.

Ironically, Winnicott's view of the self may be interpreted as relatively optimistic. He believes that there is a true self in all of us. Of course, it may be more deeply buried and inaccessible in some individuals than in others. For Winnicott, however, the true self is capable of surviving, in a repressed form, the most depriving and unloving of family environments. That means that intentionality and personal responsibility are lost forever. This is better appreciated by the introduction of the psychological model of personal responsibility in the workplace (see Chapter 3). This model provides for varied true and false self-responses to stress and anxiety.

PERSONAL RESPONSIBILITY AND THE LARGER CONTEXT

The observations of historian Christopher Lasch (1979, 1984) and psychoanalysts Heinz Kohut (1971, 1977, 1984), Otto Kernberg (1975, 1980), and Arnold Modell (1984), among others, acknowledge a shift in "the ecology of neuroses" as a response to historical change. Modell writes, for instance, that symptomatic neuroses were, first, replaced by character neuroses, which, in turn, were replaced by narcissistic personality disorders. Patients today are complaining of an absence of feelings and exhibit disorders of the self, low self-image, and a self-deficit or deficiency of healthy, narcissistic supplies.

These historical and clinical observations must be taken seriously by those who manage, work within, study, and consult to organizations. These perspectives suggest that people working in large organizations today require greater opportunities for feeling their self-worth than ever before.

Employees want to and are prepared to participate in the workplace to enhance their self-esteem by feeling valued and respected by their peers, subordinates, and superiors. However, the persistence of the psychologically defensive workplace and bureaucracy limits everyone's opportunities for the psychological rewards of self-fulfillment. This is underscored by the frequent use of downsizing, restructuring, and reengineering methods that strip employees of security and self-worth and reinforce top management's control over everyone. When the workplace becomes psychologically and socially defensive, it promotes ongoing narcissistic injuries to employees, who become focused on themselves and their needs. As a result, they are less willing to make sacrifices for organizational well-being, and are not encouraged to take risks and assume personal responsibility for their actions or inactions, often out of fear of being singled out and scapegoated.

In sum, organizations that encourage defensive, compliant, false personalities and discourage spontaneous, true personalities among executives and employees do not provide the psychological paycheck that employees desire. Role conformity becomes more highly valued than individuality, autonomy, and the development of self-esteem. The psychologically defensive workplace can only be transcended when people stop using psychological defenses and bureaucracy as defenses against anxiety (Diamond 1993; Baum 1987).

PERSONAL RESPONSIBILITY IN THE WORKPLACE

The psychologically defensive workplace translates into questioning whether executives and employees are responsible for their actions. Today they often deny, rationalize, and distance themselves from the negative consequences of their behavior. They all too frequently blame others, such as colleagues, subordinates, bosses, the system, competitors, the government, fate, or God. Blaming others externalizes responsibility for bad self-feelings, such as shame or guilt for one's contribution to or passive participation in workplace events that create negative outcomes. However, the assumption of personal responsibility is necessary for individual and organizational learning and development, and for what is, at times, maintaining the thin veneer of civilization.

Employees cannot improve upon their present circumstances, individually and organizationally, without claiming ownership of their actions (or inactions). They cannot overcome feelings of powerlessness and helplessness without assuming responsibility for their destiny. In order to reverse the perception of themselves as passive actors, recipients, and even victims of events and the actions of others, they must learn to be more reflective and intentional in order to be able to assume personal responsibility for their thoughts, feelings, and actions.

Intentionality is central to the assumption of personal responsibility. Intentionality is a way of knowing reality, as well as an ability to see and construct the future (May 1977). It means people are always moving toward something and that they are always engaged in making meaning through their actions.

Intentionality involves meditation, deliberation, and reflection upon oneself and one's situation. It is, therefore, a reflexive action that results in self-awareness and insight, and requires acknowledging one's conscious and unconscious motives, expectations, and wishes (Diamond 1985). When viewed from a clinical and theoretical perspective, being intentional means participating in the world, as well as observing it and oneself. Intentional actions require self-cohesion and a sense of one's true self (Kohut 1977; Winnicott 1965). Intentional acts, in turn, reinforce ego strength (Fenichel 1954), self-esteem, and personal integrity by merging unconscious motives and intentions with conscious awareness and actions.

In sum, the assumption of personal responsibility rests upon greater self-awareness and reflective practice, but it is not so easily achieved (Schon 1983). Most organizations discourage spontaneity and encourage compliance because they rely upon the hierarchical, control-oriented features of the psychologically defensive workplace. Those who lead them defend themselves from anxiety and conserve their power by promoting rationality, suppressing feelings, and discouraging risk-taking experimentation and change. In their place, they insist upon unilateral, top-down control, creating a dependent and anxious workforce that possesses low self-esteem. Anyone who deviates (perhaps by achieving excellence) and questions what is going on may be labeled as "not being a team player" and ostracized, isolated, and cut-off from being effective (Allcorn 1991). Not surprisingly, under these conditions the assumption of personal responsibility among workers is problematic.

THE CASE OF PERFECT CONTROL

The psychologically defensive workplace is illustrated by an organization where it was a common practice for project managers to bring three or more assistant directors of project support areas to meetings with the managing director. These assistant directors were required by the director to sign off on all expense authorizations before he did. In order to avoid excessive sign-off delays and the endless passing back and forth of the requests for further clarification, the project managers learned that, to get anything done, they had to get everyone together at the same time. The assistant directors reluctantly cooperated in this tiresome ritual of trying to control every aspect of decision making to avoid error and possible blame.

In this case, the managing director predictably defended the process on the basis that it served to avoid what could be the chief executive officer's terrible swift sword of personal accountability for a poor decision. Perfect control of all decisions was achieved at the cost of endless, time-consuming scrutiny. Should a problem still occur, incorporating as many others as possible in the approval process allowed others to be readily scapegoated, thereby further protecting the managing director from personal responsibility (Allcorn 1989a).

Everyone in the organization understood the importance of avoiding mistakes and being subjected to scapegoating by senior management. This was very clear for the project managers who were the first to be associated with a problem. They also implicitly knew that the cumbersome and frustrating process protected them, as everyone stood to get blamed if the decision "blew up." In effect, they tacitly colluded to support it, although they did work to speed it up.

This example illustrates a typical organizational outcome when avoidance of personal responsibility leads to an extraordinarily exacting, slow, frustrating, cumbersome, and alienating process of review and approval encouraged by a remote and punitive top management. The actions of all concerned are taken too far and unconsciously become a defensive routine that encourages an excessively bureaucratic structure and norms of self-protection from blame (Jaques 1955; Menzies 1960). In contrast, the willingness of organization participants to bear the anxiety associated with assuming personal responsibility for decisions is a yardstick for assessing the integrity of an organization's leadership and the organization as a whole, and thereby its potential for accomplishing work, tolerating change, and promoting development.

In sum, variations in the presence of a safe holding environment in the workplace and adequate self-esteem lead to workers experiencing stressful workplace events with differing degrees of distress, anxiety, and reliance upon psychological and bureaucratic defenses. The impact of stressful change upon an employee and his or her ability to respond responsibly depends upon the quality of each employee's autonomy, self-esteem, and psychologically defensive tendencies. The presence of autonomy and self-worth on a consistent basis is, however, questionable, which contributes to the problematic nature of the assumption of personal responsibility. In the example just given, change did not occur until several project managers complained to a new senior executive about their lack of authority and support crippling their efforts to be more effective. Change was implemented that supported their assumption of personal responsibility for approving many of the needed changes without review in order to complete projects on time and within budget.

SUMMARY

This chapter explained the problematic aspects of workers assuming personal responsibility for their thoughts, feelings, and actions in the psychologically defensive workplace. The ability to sustain intentionality, self-reflection, and learning in the face of distressing and occasionally overwhelming anxiety is readily understood to be difficult when psychologically defensive responses are unconsciously triggered. All of these aspects of the psychologically defensive workplace can be further appreciated by exploring the responses to anxiety that resemble reaction formations as described in Chapter 3. These psychologically defensive workplace practices are familiar to all of us and all too common in the workplace.

THE PSYCHOLOGICALLY DEFENSIVE SIDE OF PEOPLE AT WORK

3

Responsibility is a detachable burden easily shifted to the shoulders of God, Fate, Fortune, Luck or one's neighbor. In the days of astrology it was customary to unload it upon a star.

Bierce 1958, 112

It has been said, "Tout comprendre, c'est tout pardonner." That easy way out is not in the spirit of analysis as it is not part of the tragic sense of life. Understanding in depth seems rather to support a sense of one's own obligations and culpability and one's right to expect others to feel their obligations and culpability.

Schafer 1976, 43

The psychologically defensive workplace adversely affects the assumption of personal responsibility. This important outcome is better understood by examining a psychological model that explains how stressful workplace events trigger employee anxiety and reliance upon a system of identifiable and frequently relied upon character-like psychological defenses that, while unique to each individual, share much in common.

The degree to which executives and employees rely upon psychological defenses against workplace anxiety depends in large part upon whether their organizations promote adequate levels of security, risk taking, autonomy, self-esteem, and self-integrity, or strip them away, thereby alienating employees and executives from themselves, each other, and their work. When executives and employees experience themselves as over-controlled, vulnerable to abandonment, and, therefore, anxious, they psychologically defend themselves. These psychological defenses, which often take the form of false-self, character-like personality organizations emphasize interpersonal control and conformity over spontaneity, routine over innovation, work over play, rationality over creativity, and inauthenticity over authenticity (Masterson 1988; Winnicott 1965). What people do or not do, what they think, and how they feel (or do not think and feel) is, in large part, no longer their responsibility, but rather someone else's responsibility or the organization's responsibility. They can no longer be held accountable. These psychologically defensive dynamics are the basis for the model of the psychologically defensive workplace.

STRESS, ANXIETY, AND THE SELF AT WORK

The psychological model, as illustrated in Figure 3.1, begins with people entering the workplace with predetermined personalities, self-esteem, and ways of relating to others, including time-worn and trusted psychological defenses against anxiety. The model focuses attention upon the ability of executives and employees to avoid psychological defensiveness when the workplace becomes stressful. Critical moments, such as management downsizing, leadership transitions, audits, changes in target markets or service environments, reorganizations, rapid expansions, and public accountability are all common sources of stress.

ORGANIZATIONAL STRESS

There can be no doubt that organizational change and the interpersonal world at work are stressful. Stress in the workplace arises from uncontrollable, unpredictable, and often ambiguous events and employee interactions that are felt to be distressing because they threaten security, self-esteem, and oneself (Diamond and Allcorn 1985). The degree to which threat to self and anxiety are experienced by executives and employees depends upon the quality of their self-cohesion and self-esteem. The interaction of stress and marginal employee self-integration and self-esteem can result in crippling fear and anxiety that leads to the emergence of the false-self, character-like psychologically defensive practices (perfectionistic, arrogant–vindictive, narcissistic, self-effacing, and resigned) described in this chapter. In sum, organizational stressors, if experienced as excessively threatening to oneself and one's self-esteem, trigger psychologically defensive reactions among executives and employees that adversely affect their ability to continue to assume personal responsibility.

Anxiety

The model of the psychologically defensive workplace makes a distinction between normal and neurotic anxiety. Rollo May (1977) describes normal

Figure 3.1
Model of Psychologically Defensive Workplace Practices

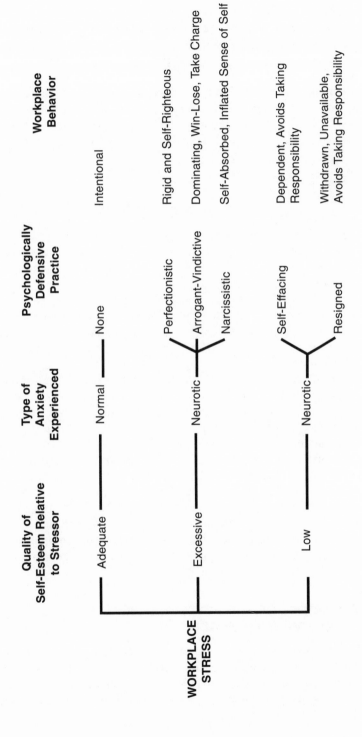

anxiety as a reaction to stress that is not disproportionate to the objective threat and does not involve repression or other psychologically defensive mechanisms for managing intrapsychic conflict. In contrast, May (1977) describes neurotic anxiety as a reaction that is disproportionate to the threat, because intrapsychic conflict is involved. Neurotic anxiety occurs when the experience of the stressful event becomes highly threatening to oneself. The threat becomes personalized and subjective and dominated by inner conflicts that make executives and employees overly anxious, thereby provoking psychological defensiveness that inhibits them from being entirely intentional.

Self-Esteem

Self-esteem is defined as the value (positive or negative) one consistently places upon oneself. The origins of self-esteem arise from "good enough" parenting in the form of sufficient mirroring and idealization in the parent–infant dyad, where interpersonal security and self-cohesion are developed (Kohut 1977; Sullivan 1953; Winnicott 1965). Adequate self-esteem encourages realization of a true self which possess minimal intrapsychic conflict.

However, experience of what Winnicott (1965) calls an infant's holding environment as anxiety ridden, insecure, hostile, and uncertain results in damage to self-esteem and the creation of basic anxiety (Horney 1950) and a false self. Variations in individual levels of self-esteem relative to various stressors, and the presence, to varying degrees, of true or false selves among organization members, will, at times, trigger excessive anxiety and fear when stressful events occur. False-self, character-like compromise and reaction formations, and accompanying psychological defenses that support them (psychologically defensive practices), then emerge to distort reality testing and compromise intentionality. It should be noted that in a large group some, if not many, group members may become anxious at the same time, thereby promoting a collective resort to reliance upon familiar and often similar psychological defenses. This outcome accounts for unusual and often irresponsible acts by the group, because its members become psychologically defensive. Group members may stop at nothing to gain control of others and the situation, including developing an alternate reality, as occurs in "group think." Removing the stress and allaying their distressing experience of anxiety becomes a paramount but unconscious group dynamic.

THE MODEL OF THE PSYCHOLOGICALLY DEFENSIVE WORKPLACE

Karen Horney's (1950) categories of neurotic solutions to anxiety inform the following discussion of five psychologically defensive practices in the workplace. The defensive practices also implicitly incorporate and are supported by the psychological defenses described in Chapter 1. Appendix 1 is provided to further illustrate the relationship of these defensive practices to the psychological defenses.

The first three psychologically defensive practices share expansive tendencies to master and control events and people in order to allay anxiety. The remaining two psychologically defensive practices complement these expansive tendencies by introducing contrasting dependent and withdrawn psychologically defensive practices.

Introduction to the Model

The dynamics of the model begin with a stressful incident, such as the announcement of another round of downsizing and reengineering. Some employees greet the announcement with concern, but they do not feel excessively threatened and normal anxiety arises, permitting reflection on the meaning and implications of the announcement. Intentionality is maintained and these employees respond to the announcement as a challenge to learn, change, and develop themselves and the organization.

For others, the announcement is experienced as threatening to their more fragile sense of self-esteem. To some extent, these employees unconsciously fused their self-esteem to having their job and receiving approval for their work. As a result, it is important that they control others and their work in order to feel good about themselves (maintain their self-image and self-esteem). However, in this case, since their ability to control events is minimal, the employees begin to psychologically protect themselves rather than deal with the impending downsizing. They respond to the announcement in ways that alleviate their anxiety about themselves and their self-esteem. They unconsciously split themselves into idealized and despised images, retaining one of the images and projecting the dispossessed image onto others. They may also avoid the experience altogether, by withdrawing and repressing the true self.

Identification with the idealized image leads to character-like expansive solutions to anxiety, including the perfectionistic, arrogant–vindictive, and narcissistic psychologically defensive practices (Horney 1950). Identification with the despised self-image results in the self-effacing psychologically defensive practice. In this case, rather than clinging to an idealized, controlling, commanding, admirable, and near-perfect self-image, the experience of anxiety confirms the employee's low self-esteem and feelings of being inadequate, helpless, and worthless. Tendencies toward self-minimization, self-discounting, and self-denigration emerge to reinforce self-experience as being inadequate.

Finally, some executives and employees may respond to the announcement by avoidance and withdrawal. They repress or suppress their awareness, thoughts, and feelings (elements of an active life) to some extent. They may report having not heard of the announcement or appear to have misunderstood it and its significance. At the same time, they may stop interacting with others.

These executives and employees take flight from the stressful environment by retreating into the self. They report that they just want to be left alone to do their work. It must be added that these psychologically defensive workplace practices are found in combination with each other, because they are often used in a sequence. Also to be noted is that the resigned defensive practice is often resorted to when the other two defensive practices do not allay anxiety or are not available to the individual. These provisos are to be kept in mind any time the model is used to understand the workplace.

The Idealized Psychologically Defensive Practices

The Perfectionistic Practice   It is striking how often perfectionistic tendencies are found in bureaucratic organizations because they are so compatible with bureaucratic preoccupation with perfecting control over all aspects of work life. Perfectionists have a superior and controlling attitude and like to pay close attention to detail. Identification with a perfectionistic ego ideal or the perfect organizational ideal (Schwartz 1990), or what is referred to here as the idealized self, results in the compulsive pursuit of perfection for its own sake. These pursuits lead to the imposition of perfect standards upon others who cannot meet them, which makes the perfectionist feel superior. Perfectionists who try to meet their own perfect standards result in executives or employees who are preoccupied with micromanaging and controlling themselves, everyone, and everything in order to achieve absolute perfection according to these standards. As a result, perfectionists tend to be rigid and unaccepting of others, their work, and change. Their constant and compulsive pursuit of perfect control and performance according to their own subjective standards is the only thing that matters. By comparison, the imposition of the same life- and joy-draining standards upon others invariably shows them to be imperfect and inferior to the perfectionist (who holds the standards), which boosts the perfectionist's self-esteem. The perfectionist is compelled to be constantly critical of the others.

In the workplace, executives often deny group conflicts and performance problems. They often attribute problems to others (scapegoats) and feel as though only they should be in control. When these actions are viewed from a psychological perspective, it is understood that these executives split off their imperfect parts and project them onto their staff. As a result, the executives feel better about themselves and superior to their staff. Subordinates are, consequently, forced to rationalize, deny, and suppress acknowledgement of their many failures and problems and the accompanying anger over how they are being treated. The executive's punitive, anxious, and judgmental reactions to problems and scapegoating of others make it clear that something is wrong, which encourages wholesale repression and suppression of feelings on the part of the staff. It is not uncommon to find instances where executives have yelled at and humiliated employees for making a mistake. These employees and their colleagues quickly learn that they must be perfect to avoid being scapegoated and publicly humiliated. The result is that the pursuit of perfection and the denial of imperfection (covering it up) promotes defensiveness between management and staff and the avoidance of learning needed to improve organizational performance. Employees know that the perfection expected by the executive is impossible to achieve and that it sets them up to fail. Approval is either withheld or provided with the proviso that next-time performance will be even better. As a result, employees experience themselves to be in an anger-filled double bind (where they must also manage their feelings), which is especially acute for those who also possess perfectionist tendencies.

Ironically, the perfectionist ideal blocks the ability of the perfectionist to learn by detecting and correcting errors. The perfectionist believes that, due to his or her superiority over others, he or she cannot and should not be held personally accountable when something goes wrong. This results in scapegoating and endless criticizing of others who do not meet the perfectionist's standards. In sum, if the perfectionist acknowledges fault, his or her defensive and compensatory view of self as flawless, in control, and incapable of mistakes is threatened, thereby provoking more anxiety and an ever greater pursuit of perfection and control. The discovery of problems, therefore, does not produce learning on the part of the perfectionist. Rather, their discovery reinforces the perfectionist's attitude that others are inferior and imperfect. These attributes of the perfectionist, as well as the remaining types of defensive practices, are summarized in Figure 3.2.

The Arrogant–Vindictive Practice It is often said that bureaucratic institutions bring out the worst in people (Argyris 1957; Denhardt 1981; Diamond 1984; Hummel 1977; LaBier 1986; Maccoby 1976; Sperling 1950). Arrogant–vindictive practices are characterized by those who show contempt for others and believe that only they can supervise or perform the work properly. Similar to the perfectionist, the arrogant–vindictive executive or employee identifies with an idealized self that is all knowing and powerful and believes that only he or she can design, do, or supervise the work properly and should therefore be in absolute control. As a result, this employee has an arrogant and superior attitude toward others who are seen as inferior. At the same time, this individual feels that he or she is not particularly likeable (unlovable as a child) and has nothing to lose by bullying, intimidating and alienating others. Anyone who challenges this executive's or employee's superior self-concept becomes the target of vindictive aggression, where winning at any cost is the only thing that matters.

This psychologically defensive practice results in work not being valued for its own sake. Work and the workplace become a battleground where intimidation and the exploitation of others becomes acceptable (Diamond and Allcorn 1985). The predominant attitude toward work and others is win or

Figure 3.2
Attributes of the Intentional Practice and Psychologically Defensive Practice Types

THE INTENTIONAL PRACTICE	THE PERFECTIONISTIC PRACTICE	THE ARROGANT-VINDICTIVE PRACTICE
Self-reflective and questions what is going on and why. Willing to advocate for a point of view but knows when to compromise. Collaborative, participative, spontaneous, creative, risk taking, and rejects routinization and bureaucracy. Good follower or leader and will delegate, which does not threaten self-esteem.	Imposes hard-to-meet standards and expects others to meet them. Self-righteous, hyper-critical, and highly judgmental of others. Projects an image of superiority. Does not accept criticism but eagerly condemns others for not meeting the imposed standards. Deprives staff of approval as their work is never quite perfect. Obsessed with control of others, work, and detail (micromanagement). Does not delegate. May become exhausted from trying to meet self-imposed standards for performance.	Highly competitive and must win all encounters at any cost. Intent upon defeating and humiliating others who harm arrogant pride. Usual expectations of ethical and moral behavior may be put aside in the pursuit of victory. Deceitful and manipulative as needed to win. Suspicious of others who are often felt to be a threat. Does not delegate and is contemptuous of others. May openly wish to replace a superior. Paralyzes others with fear by being intimidating.

lose, triumph or defeat, self-aggrandizement or self-annihilation. The experience of being evaluated by others, held accountable, or defeated, is intolerable. It threatens this individual's arrogant pride and produces anger and resentment that surface as overt or disguised aggression directed against others, especially those perceived to be the source of the humiliation (Diamond and Allcorn 1985). When change or a problem is detected in the workplace, psychologically defensive arrogant–vindictive workplace practices necessitate moving quickly and forcefully to reestablish mastery over others and the situation. Included among the actions to regain power and control are scapegoating others and striking back at anyone who attempts to associate this individual with responsibility for the problem. At times, the level of aggression and the amount of risk assumed in order to win a conflict can be both intimidating (even to superiors) and attention getting. The person may seem

Figure 3.2 (continued)

THE NARCISSISTIC PRACTICE	THE SELF-EFFACING PRACTICE	THE RESIGNED PRACTICE
Projects an image of self-confidence and demands admiration and loyalty from others. Dreamer and risk taker but prefers to avoid the details of actually carrying out the work. Develops big ideas and plans which are accompanied by boundless energy. Often works on many projects and may shift from one to the other without bringing any to fruition. Can be manipulative, autocratic, and scapegoat others when problems occur. Does not delegate.	Prefers to be dependent and follow orders, plans, and regulations. Wants to be liked and taken care of by others in return for being supportive of them. Often appears to be a helpless, powerless, vulnerable victim who needs caretaking. May invite being taken advantage of by others who are willing to take charge. Willingly delegates to be rid of responsibility. Is a master of being flexible, adaptive, and identifying ways to be ingratiating to others. Steadfastly avoids accepting responsibility.	Prefers to be left alone and avoids performance goals which are experienced as a coercive influence. Constantly avoids being subordinated and is in frequent conflict with authority figures. Is mistrustful of others who are felt to be controlling. Dumps responsibility upon rather than meaningfully delegating it to others. Avoids relationships and competition, preferring rather to be isolated and aloof. Can be nonadaptive, rebellious, and seldom offers any type of leadership.

self-righteous and greatly offended and feel fully empowered to do whatever is needed to vindicate the harm done, regain control, and set things right. As a result of the level of aggression displayed, others may avoid confronting this individual, which has the unintended outcome of rewarding the behavior, as it is successful in obtaining what is desired by the arrogant–vindictive individual. It should also be noted that this behavior is often seen as dynamic and take-charge by top management, who may reward this employee with promotions (assuming that the level of aggression remains within reasonable limits). However, promotion to positions of greater power and responsibility is problematic. These executives and employees assume responsibility only when it is linked to some organizational victory or good.

As in the case of the perfectionistic practice, the governing values and attributes of bureaucracy facilitate the psychologically defensive arrogant–vindictive practice. Bureaucratic executives often perpetuate an interpersonal and inter-departmental psychology of comparison and competition that obstructs coop-eration and teamwork. They often act with little regard to the thoughts and feelings of others by making unilateral decisions regarding resource alloca-tion. These same executives often intimidate their staff by evaluating them against perfect standards, and use their position and the organizational re-sources at their disposal to their best advantage—to get even or, better, ahead. A typical example of this kind of intraorganizational conflict involves the ma-nipulation and aggressive use of information to achieve and maintain power and fortify divisional boundaries against informed attacks and incursions.

In order to be proven right and garner approval and scarce resources, arrogant–vindictive executives and employees often perceive other executives and employees as adversaries who must be defeated. This hostile and competi-tive work setting encourages them to view each other with suspicion and mis-trust which, given time, turns into paranoia that someone else may triumph, thereby provoking a new wave of anxiety and arrogant–vindictive behavior.

The Narcissistic Practice   Mirroring and idealization between parent and child are necessary components of healthy human development. However, approval may be withheld or manipulated to control the child. When a child does not develop good self-feelings and adequate self-esteem, he or she may become dependent upon what others think, feel, and do relative to him or her. From this dependence develops a preoccupation with trying to gain the miss-ing admiration and approval from others to fulfill an idealized self-image, which is a reaction formation to the parental despised image. Adults who are excessively dependent upon others for good self feelings, self-cohesion, and glorification are not simply seeking recognition; they are narcissistic.

A narcissistic executive or employee's idealized self-image encourages fantasies of omnipotence and grandiosity. He or she wants to feel as though an adoring universe revolves around him or her. Similar to the other two ex-pansive practices, the stress caused by the uncertainty of critical incidents at work is experienced as threatening to this employee's idealized self-image. Change and problems threaten well-established roles and interpersonal rela-tionships that provide the much-needed narcissistic supplies of admiration. The narcissist is also only willing to assume responsibility when that claim reinforces his or her need for adoration and self-aggrandizement. This execu-tive or employee often tries to take responsibility for everyone and everything in the belief that only he or she can handle the work, but quickly abandons the responsibility if things do not go well. The focus upon assuming respon-sibility is usually merely a platform for the propagation of grand ideas and there is little appreciation of what it really takes to get the work done. This, if acknowledged, deflates the grandiosity. Inevitably, something goes wrong, and the narcissist denies responsibility for it. He or she will not admit to a blunder or acknowledge that he or she has been led astray by a cadre of hand-picked, admiring, unquestioning, and loyal followers. The idealized self-image must be defended at all costs.

Bureaucratic hierarchy and centralized power and authority provide a structural setting conducive to psychologically defensive narcissistic practices. Executives, in particular, often rely upon their position of authority to boost their self-esteem, which is often under pressure due to the responsibilities that they assume. In the worst-case scenario, they may require unquestioning obedience, adoration, and loyalty from their staff to inflate their worthless sense of self. Consequently, narcissistic executives misjudge their limitations and others and think nothing of involving the organization in unorthodox, risky, and even illegal ventures that exceed their authority and their administrative capabilities. These same managers also tend to ignore supervisory responsibilities and daily operating details, which may lead to unethical practices among their staff.

Staff who work with such an executive often feel depleted of good self feelings and demoralized as a result of catering to their superior's excessive demands for self-aggrandizement, which often strips them of good self feelings. All successes are attributed to the executive, often with no or token acknowledgement of the work of their staff. Predictably, problems are attributed to them. The resulting narcissistic organizational culture leaves just about everyone feeling drained of good self feelings and anxious about being scapegoated. At the same time, a small "in group" or "kitchen cabinet" that feeds the executive's narcissistic needs creates divisive interpersonal interactions and paranoia when it becomes known that these individuals report everything that they see and hear to their narcissistic boss to receive sought-after attention and approval.

The Despised Psychologically Defensive Self-Effacing Practice

Self-effacing practices are compatible with subordination. "I'm not really worthy of your respect!" and "Your needs are more important than mine!" are statements that reflect the attitudes of self-effacing employees who, when ordered to jump, respond with the only possible response, "How high?"

Rather than idealizing oneself as a defense against basic anxiety about oneself and self-worth, this executive or employee idealizes others and despises him- or herself. Despising oneself is contributed to by the holding of perfectionistic self standards that cannot be met (very likely taken in during childhood from ever-critical, judgmental, and unrewarding parents). As a result, the employee feels inferior; unworthy of being liked, respected, or admired; ineffective; and he or she abhors personal tendencies to think, feel, or act effectively or aggressively (a reaction formation). The employee prefers having little if any responsibility and authority at work. He or she steadfastly relies upon others for direction and protection from blame and anxiety-ridden situations. This executive or employee is much more comfortable in a role of dependency, where his or her needs are taken care of by powerful others. When a critical incident occurs, this executive or employee looks anxiously for others to assure him or her that he or she is still needed, that their relationship will not change, and that he or she should not worry. This at times pathetic role of dependency insures that this individual is willing to do whatever is asked of him or her as long as he or she does not have to take responsibility for how he or she thinks, feels, or acts.

Hierarchically arranged interactions encourage self-effacing practices among employees. While perfectionistic, arrogant–vindictive, and narcissistic practices are expansive psychologically defensive tendencies typically associated with executive positions, self-effacing psychologically defensive practices are common to roles of subordination and, in fact, are often the consequence of subordination to executives who act out the three expansive tendencies.

In sum, self-minimization results from both measuring one's performance against internally held perfectionistic standards and from one's superior, who may be constantly willing to find fault with everything. Subordinate denigration and self-denigration can also be a consequence of a double bind in which the employee fears producing quality work because he or she will incur the executive's envious, arrogant, and vindictive feelings associated with subordinate success (Allcorn 1991; Diamond and Allcorn 1985). In these cases, subordinates find themselves between a rock and a hard place. Poor performance justifies the executive's feelings of superiority over them, while good performance threatens the executive's self-image and elicits his or her hostility. Finally, executives who require narcissistic supplies from staff prefer self-effacing subordinates who are more than willing to fuel and inflate the executive's expansive self-image. The greater the expectations and demands of these executives, the more they are idealized by the self-effacing psychologically defensive practices of subordinates.

The Repressed Psychologically Defensive Resigned Practice

Resigned practices are also found among executives and subordinates, but they are invariably detrimental to organizational performance when executives act them out. This psychologically defensive practice leads organizational members to withdraw from active participation in operations and workplace relationships by physically and emotionally distancing themselves from painful aspects of organizational life when they encounter distressing organizational events. At these times, they prefer to be left alone and feel that the attempts by others to get them to take charge, direct their work, or get them involved are coercive (Diamond and Allcorn 1985). It is also important to note that this psychologically defensive practice is often relied upon when the executive or employee is unable to experience him- or herself in an idealized expansive or resigned dependent way. These practices may be unavailable or abhorred, thereby leaving psychological withdrawal as the last recourse to minimize anxiety.

In the workplace, some employees take flight from stressful circumstances. They run for emotional shelter to hide from the coercive intentions of others. The resigned employee is able to do so mostly in his or her mind and, to some degree, in his or her actions. In contrast to the psychological splitting of the self into two parts (one idealized and one despised), this employee represses the self and psychologically withdraws from him- or herself, others, stressful workplace events, and work life in general. Autonomy and freedom from coercive interactions of others is valued over all else and takes the form of psychological distancing from others and events. This employee prefers that others work it out for themselves and does not want to assume responsibility for the effects that his or her withdrawal have upon others and the organization.

Executives who are uncomfortable with confronting problems and resolving conflicts often retreat to their offices and leave staff to fend for themselves. These executives appear to be puzzled and unwilling to assume personal responsibility. Their bureaucratic positions of authority, however, enable them to maintain a safe distance. As a result, mistrust and suspicion among employees develops in the leadership void. Turf battles, in-fighting, the withholding of information, and the manipulation of organizational resources accelerate. Resigned executives further reinforce organizational dynamics by suppressing conflict and denying that turmoil exists, which eventually results in less than effective organizational performance and higher levels of anxiety, further reinforcing their tendency to withdraw.

Each psychologically defensive practice is an attempt to protect the executive or employee from anxiety and, in turn, assures that personal growth and organizational development are limited. In sum, psychologically defensive practices create a self-sealing and self-perpetuating system of thinking, feeling, and acting, insuring that intentionality, learning, and change are unlikely. It must also be noted that executives and employees will primarily rely upon one of these practices but may, with the right provocation, temporarily rely upon one or more of the other practices in rapid succession or concurrently in order to achieve their goal of alleviating internal conflict and anxiety spawned by stressful workplace conditions.

SUMMARY

This chapter has explained that the maintenance of intentionality and the assumption of personal responsibility by organization members is problematic. Employees who report that they abhor the alienating features of rigidly controlled, psychologically defensive, and cumbersome hierarchical bureau-cratic organizations often unintentionally act to perpetuate these features by acting out psychologically defensive practices to avoid anxiety. Organization members learn to act in ways that, while adaptive to organizational life (not necessarily organizational well-being), estrange them from feeling responsible out of fear of being humiliated or scapegoated. Their false, psychologically defensive workplace self, the way they have to act to be a "good" employee and a "team player," takes over.

This chapter has operationalized this loss of intentionality and responsibil-ity by presenting a model of the psychologically defensive workplace. The five psychologically defensive practices illustrate how what may appear to be natural and adaptive work-related behavior can also be understood to be part of an unacknowledged and undiscussable system of defensive behavior aimed at minimizing anxiety and avoiding personal responsibility.

THE PSYCHOLOGICALLY DEFENSIVE SIDE OF THE INTERPERSONAL WORLD AT WORK

4

Managing People and Roles

For us, role has a behavioral point of reference, expressing the individual's personality as much as, sometimes more than, the expectations of others in the organization.

> Hodgson, Levinson, and Zaleznik 1965, 30

Taking a role should not be confused with play-acting on the stage. The conscious and deliberate enactment of a role as a theatrical performance is bound in time and, although it involves the individual, it is a highly limited performance. Role-taking in organizations is part and parcel of character structure, the habitual modes of responding to internal and external stimuli. Therefore, the individual's performance serves defensive as well as adaptive purposes.

> Zaleznik and Kets de Vries 1985, 34

Executives and employees enter the psychologically defensive workplace with preestablished levels of self-esteem, psychological defenses, and dependable, character-like, psychologically defensive practices that enable them to cope more or less effectively with daily work life. All of these virtually unacknowledged personal attributes and tendencies, however, are inevitably acted out relative to others, who are frequently the source of the anxiety. Individual and interpersonal dynamics are so complex that it is hard to understand them without a suitable theoretical frame of reference. The one used here to understand interpersonal behavior in the psychologically defensive workplace is *role,* which links individual psychologically defensive tendencies to actions relative to others in the workplace.

ROLES IN THE WORKPLACE

The assignment of roles as documented in job descriptions is intended by management to coordinate work and organize and empower employees to perform work. It is equally clear that employees often unilaterally modify their assigned roles as a part of their natural desire to do work that they enjoy and do it in ways that fit their personalities and personal preferences. As a result, formal organizational roles are usually enacted by employees who, at least in part, use them to meet personal needs rather than fulfill organizational interests. Workplace roles can, therefore, be understood to be more complex than the traditional notion of written job descriptions. In fact, roles consist of a combination of hard-to-understand and manage-conscious and -unconscious intrapsychic and interpersonal dimensions that do not always contribute to individual, interpersonal, group, and organizational competence. Executives and employees often use roles to try to control their work and the thoughts, feelings, and actions of others to minimize anxiety associated with workplace ambiguity and, in particular, interpersonal relations. In sum, workplace roles are used to operationalize the character-like, psychologically defensive practices.

Anxious workers regularly step out of their assigned roles to create psychologically defensive workplace relations. Shapiro and Carr write

By creating, managing, and developing a shared task, one function of organizations and institutions is to provide a holding environment similar to that first experienced in the family. But just as such holding is negotiated in the family, so, too, is that provided by organizations. Members can create these holding qualities through the negotiation of a shared culture in which the individual's experience as articulated through his organizational role is assumed to illuminate underlying values, characteristics, or assumptions of the organization. (1991, 77)

Organizational roles may, therefore, be understood to, like family roles, represent a Winnicottian holding environment: containing feelings of aggression and intimacy so that they may be acknowledged and shared safely, and in a way that is consistent with the common task (Winnicott 1965).

The holding environment, whether between mother and infant or among organizational members, absorbs and minimizes anxieties so that development, play, and work are possible. For the crawling infant, a good enough mother (who it is not feared will abandon or punish her child for autonomous behavior) enables him or her to explore his or her world and learn. In effect, the infant's curiosity, capacity for learning, and willingness to experiment develop out of this nurturing matrix.

Similarly, work roles (with their clear organizational placement, role-to-role boundaries, and task responsibilities) facilitate collaborative problem solving and reflective action in organizations, which, in turn, permits the discovery and inventiveness necessary for learning. However, if role clarity is lacking or if roles become rigid and restricting and permit no sense of autonomy or self-expression, the prerequisites for a safe holding environment are compromised and potentially crippling abandonment or engulfment anxiety arises. In these instances, unconsciously negotiated and unacknowledged anxiety-reducing interpersonal expectations often govern role performance by employees. As a result, when the holding environment at work fails, conflict-ridden working relationships develop that lead to organizational dysfunction. Mistrust and suspicion develop among workers which further promotes basic anxiety and turns them away from constructive confrontation and role and task clarification. This defective work bond, similar to the mother–infant bond in the holding environment, fails to eliminate (or minimize) the organizational members' abandonment (separation) or engulfment (autonomy) anxiety and, consequently, perpetuates their anxieties and associated psychologically defensive practices.

In sum, the ritualistic, unreflective, and psychologically defensive aspects of organizational life compromise formal organizational roles. Roles become the outcome of employee unconscious adjustment to the stressful demands of organizational life, horizontal and vertical relationships and expectations, and the need to maintain ego integrity and self-esteem.

Howard Stein (1986) refers to the psychodynamics of social roles as "unconscious complementarity." He suggests that projective identification has a central function in the formation of workplace roles when work bonds are flawed and the holding environment is inadequate. Therefore, to more fully understand work roles, one must examine their social and individual context. This psychosocial perspective offers valuable insight into the case of Joe Smith and his role. The following case, formulated from interviews, illustrates the unconscious dimensions of role performance in organizations.

THE CASE OF JOE SMITH, VICE PRESIDENT FOR OPERATIONS

Joe Smith, vice president for operations, when asked about his role defined it precisely as the vice president for operations (see Figure 4.1). His response is understood to mean that he supervises managers below him in the organizational hierarchy, which implies that they are accountable to him. In fact, his role, as defined by his job description, attested to that interpretation and it is what Joe tells new employees so that everyone explicitly understands Joe's role. Joe is in charge. However, despite this clarity, Joe does not actually try to supervise anyone. Those who report to him only come to him for information and otherwise function autonomously. His leadership style, however, has

Figure 4.1
Roles as Unconscious Mutual Concessions

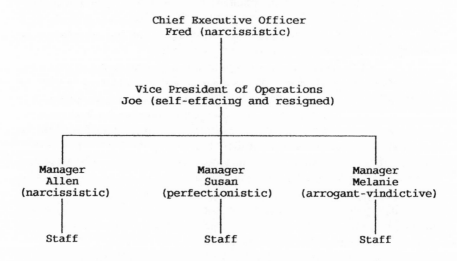

led to a number of hard-to-resolve operating problems. Rather than deal with them, he has retreated to the sanctity and safety of his office, leaving the problems for someone else to deal with.

Joe appears to be paralyzed and unable to act during stressful periods even though he is a VP and possesses considerable knowledge and expertise. Joe acts as though he fears that the exercise of his formal authority will threaten Fred (Chief Executive Officer), his boss, and hurt others. As a result, he does not take authoritative steps and the problems get worse. He then spends more and more time closeted in his office. This has resulted in the inability of the operations division to carry out complex tasks because there is a lack of planning, coordination, and follow through. These operating frustrations have resulted in considerable conflict and, more recently, frequent incursions by Fred to straighten out problems in Joe's areas of responsibility. How can the discrepancy between Joe's formal role (he is the boss) and how it is operationalized (he is not the boss) be understood?

Analysis of Joe's Role

Joe's role performance, it may be understood, is governed by elements of several of the psychologically defensive practices. Joe clearly wants to feel powerful and admired (the narcissistic psychologically defensive practice). He is, after all, a vice president, which is an important title, and he does tell everyone who works for him that he is in charge. However, at the same time, he is fearful that he will lose the affection of those who work with him if he begins to assert the power contained in his position and give them direct instructions (the self-effacing psychologically defensive practice). In fact, while he likes the attention and power his position provide him, he also hates to be seen as being bossy. This is obviously a dilemma for which he has no solution. Paradoxically, if he does not eventually act powerfully he risks losing the respect and confidence his staff have for him to lead them in their work. Joe, therefore, experiences an irreconcilable double bind.

Unable to resolve the contradictions and take charge of things without feeling bossy and hypercritical, Joe retreated from active engagement in managing and problem solving (the resigned psychological defensive practice). He became less visible in the plant and in meetings and retreated to within the protective shelter of his office and official role. For the most part, he abandoned the pursuit of being powerful, admired, and liked, which became mutually exclusive pursuits when major operating problems developed. It was simply easier and safer for Joe to withdraw into a protective shell and hope to be left alone. In sum, Joe's conflicted wishes, needs, and fears dominate his actions at work. The result has been an ever-increasing number of operating problems and unresolved conflicts, which are threatening the company and have led to numerous interventions by Fred.

Awareness of Joe's psychologically defensive practices enacted through his role permits us to empathize with Joe and gain insight into the unconscious dynamics of his personality, a personality that shapes the workplace and which, in turn, is shaped by the workplace. This in-depth understanding of the interrelatedness of intrapsychic, interpersonal, group, and organizational dynamics forms the basis for potentially repairing the dysfunctional working relationships that have arisen in operations.

Understanding Joe's paradoxical behavior begins by acknowledging that Joe's role is part of a larger social system of roles, expectations, and tasks. His role performance depends upon others, including the CEO, the managers who report to him, and their staff. In this case, the fact that he does not act to directly manage anyone is a consequence of numerous unspoken compromises between him, Fred, and other organizational members, which means that Joe is not solely responsible for his role and its performance. He shares that responsibility with others. The fact that managers do not expect Joe to assign them tasks signifies the presence of an undiscussed interpersonal agenda about organizational power and authority. The managers desire autonomy and Joe wishes to appear important, but he also wants to be likable in their eyes. He therefore avoids using the power and authority of his role to tell anyone what to do. In sum, the interpersonal and role relationships in which Joe functions have a combined influence that creates problems of accountability created by the ambiguity of the unclear and, to some degree, unconsciously formed and tacitly accepted and enacted roles.

Joe is part of an organized system or matrix of role relationships. He depends upon these role relationships for security against the anxieties associated with fears of abandonment and engulfment. His relationships, therefore, become a socially defensive system that contain hard to balance and resolve conflict between his wish to be powerful and authoritative and his desire to be liked, secure, and protected. Joe's solution to this anxiety-ridden conflict is to withdraw, which is yet another unconscious compromise that enables him to be in a position of authority without assuming responsibility and the associated risks of taking charge and alienating others.

In sum, the complexity of human nature and the interpersonal world creates many interlocking role relationships. Everyone needs security. Each individual's psychologically defensive role enactment is intricately interwoven through those of others to become the organization. The use of this metaphor stresses the complexity of psychological and organizational dynamics as represented by a host of conscious and unconscious role constellations. Joe's interpretation of his role is understood to be supported by those of his colleagues, who also want to be powerful and autonomous and, at the same time, loved and taken care of. These interpersonal and role-to-role interactions are further understood by examining Joe's relationship to Fred and his three immediate subordinates: Allen, Susan, and Melanie.

Role Analysis: Projective Identification at Work

The knee-jerk response of observers and organizational members to the situation described might be to blame Joe for the operating deficiencies and terminate him. Many organizations deal with similar problems in just this way and never fully comprehend why the problems persist, despite new management, long after the sacrifice of the scapegoat.

However, firing Joe may also be part of a larger social phenomenon. Blaming and scapegoating are a consequence of the unconscious processes of splitting off and subsequently projecting bad feelings (anger, hostility, and frustrations) onto someone else. Organizational members momentarily feel better and convince themselves that they have solved their problems by ridding themselves of the "bad" member or members who caused the problems. However, these actions do not contribute to organizational learning, collaboration, and problem solving. They are counterproductive and defensive responses to the stress and anxiety caused by awareness of operating difficulties. The problem of Joe's role enactment, it must therefore be acknowledged, is also the responsibility of the members of his role constellation and their unconscious mutual interpersonal concessions. These unconscious aspects of Joe's relationships with the CEO and key players in operations must be explained before a full understanding of what is happening can be developed. In particular, their mutually developed psychologically defensive practices and their impact upon individual roles and expectations, task assignments, and organizational performance must be elaborated.

There are two central questions: To what extent is Joe's enactment of his role unconsciously determined by him and subsequently reinforced by unconscious elements of role selection and performance by his CEO and the managers who report to him? How do these intrapersonal and interpersonal dynamics affect organizational dynamics?

Joe and Fred

Joe's boss, Fred, is in charge of the organization which he has single-handily built into a major corporation. Fred defines his job as being primarily political. He must deal with other vice presidents, the Board of Directors, other CEOs, and the public. Joe respects and admires Fred, who hired him three years ago to run the business, but he is also intimidated by Fred, who periodically launches into public tirades against him and his colleagues when production difficulties are encountered (the arrogant–vindictive psychologically defensive practice). As a result, he has never asked Fred for explicit empowerment, fearing punishment and rejection from Fred, and little has been offered by Fred. Joe, at times, merely seems to be Fred's surrogate and not really in charge. As a result, Joe's managers feel that they should work independently of Joe, who they feel is not really in charge and divisional linkages and coordination of tasks have suffered.

These interpersonal dynamics can be further explored from the point of view that psychologically defensive practices are at work. Fred likes his power and the politics. He revels in working closely with the Board President. Nevertheless, he is suspicious of others (who he fears will take power from him), which reinforces his reliance upon the arrogant–vindictive psychologically defensive practice. Fred is rarely in the office during the day. He spends most of his time traveling around the country to meet with his peers, and he expects Joe to handle things in his absence. However, Fred has never explicitly delegated the necessary authority to enable Joe to be effective. He acts as though Joe is in charge, yet he routinely directly contacts Joe's managers who are working on his pet projects, which publically undermines Joe's ability to manage. Despite Fred's absence and limited day-to-day contact, he is, in effect, unwilling to relinquish control of projects that he is interested in. In fact, he relishes the aggrandizement of these managers. As a result, overall coordination of roles, tasks, communications, and planning suffer. The managers often fight over unclear jurisdictional boundaries, withhold information from each other, and aggressively compete for scarce resources, including Fred's attention.

Fred's "hands-on" oversight of his favorite projects makes him feel good (powerful and in control). He wants to be in charge and to look good to the Board, the community, and his employees. However, while his psychologically defensive practice works for him, it clearly generates problems for his organization. His employees fear him, and those who do get to work closely with him have become his unquestioning loyal followers. Working with Fred is viewed as prestigious and, as a result, they compete with one another for Fred's time and recognition (which he tacitly encourages), which flatters Fred. This competition for attention generates mistrust among the managers and resistance to coordinating tasks and resources. In a sense, it may be understood that Fred is unconsciously recreating the same type of psychologically defensive practices that he relies upon himself (arrogant–vindictive) among his subordinates. Initially, Joe only entered the picture at times of severe conflict and his efforts at mediation among the managers were usually unsuccessful because he was not forceful enough. His preference gradually became one of not getting involved, so his continued efforts at management and mediation are superficial.

However, Fred has time limitations. He works with managers only when the situation, as he explains it, demands it. He wants it his way, but often does not appreciate that his direct orders create scheduling conflicts. When his orders create problems, he usually does not want to deal with them or harshly intervenes to correct ("You stupid fools"). This means that managers also see Fred to be, at times, like Joe—undependable and not available to help when needed, which frustrates them. Rather than expressing this frustration and anger to Fred, which is far too dangerous, they displace it onto one another and onto Joe, which is safer. Joe now steadfastly refuses to fill the leadership voids created by Fred's interventions into operations. He prefers to avoid Fred's painfully castrating incursions into his efforts to lead his staff by avoiding the risk altogether. Joe also avoids confronting Fred about the role ambiguity Fred is creating and, in doing so, denies himself the opportunity to act out his role responsibly. Nonetheless, he continues to tell others that he is in charge, which fulfills some of his need to feel important.

Joe and the Managers

Joe and Fred's psychologically defensive practices have created a psychologically defensive workplace. Their actions and conflicted unconscious motivations affect their roles in relation to each other, and it is now possible to see how their role performances are influencing the rest of the organization. Before discussing these roles, it should be remembered that all of the actors described here comprise a *role matrix*. This means that they share responsibility for production of the matrix and its performance consequences. The intention here is to explain how to render conscious the unconscious psychologically defensive dynamics of this role matrix, so that, if it were shared with management and employees, they may choose to change it rather than continue to perpetuate a dysfunctional system of roles enactments and interpersonal relationships that compromises organizational performance.

Joe and Allen

These psychologically defensive dynamics are observed in the way Fred works with Allen's unit which, it is felt by many, is special because he and his people travel abroad. Their work is perceived as glamorous, and other staff members envy him and his staff and are particularly sensitive to the fact that Allen and his group receive a lot of Fred's attention. Allen is also in charge of several of Fred's highly visible and sensitive projects. Consequently, Allen frequently bypasses Joe and reports directly to Fred. Allen shares information with Fred on politically sensitive undertakings but, because of the ambiguity and lack of accountability created by Fred and Joe, he often keeps Joe and Fred in the dark about many of his activities, thereby providing himself a great deal of autonomy. Joe is aware of this problem but does not try to rectify it, even though Fred acts as if Joe is formally accountable for the behavior of his managers, including Allen.

Allen's psychologically defensive practice is narcissistic. He took the job at Fred's request, but not to be a manager as much as an international representative. He wanted to travel and enjoy special treatment from business executives in Japan and Germany. This aspect of the job serves to fulfill Allen's desire to be important, admired, and respected, and it permits him to develop grand visions of what to do with limited responsibility for carrying them out. Allen is not an operations manager and ignores the details of everyday task assignments and coordination. In response, some members of his staff try to compensate for this lack of detailed direction and, consequently, their roles have become ambiguous as they appear to be doing Allen's job.

Joe is aware of this problem but prefers not to intervene, partially out of fear of Fred defending Allen. Allen acts as though everything is fine and Fred only seems to care about progress on his pet projects in Allen's section. Hence, Allen has constructed a role for himself that fits his narcissistic need to feel special and important. Neither Fred and his arrogant–vindictive role enactment nor Joe in his resigned role enactment contradict Allen's interpretation of his role. It may, therefore, be once again observed that the role constellation, despite its ineffective nature, is formed as a consequence of an unconscious and undiscussed mutual concession among Joe, Fred, and Allen.

Joe and Susan

Susan manages the research section. She holds excessively high standards and is detail oriented (the perfectionistic psychologically defensive practice). She micromanages everyone in her section and is convinced of her superiority and their inferiority. Susan's perfectionism suppresses the talents and skills of her staff, who feel constrained but do not say anything to Susan or Joe out of fear of being criticized, attacked, or fired. They assume, and with good reason, that Susan might turn the blame back on them and Joe might tell them to work it out with Susan. Not surprisingly, they find themselves in a double-bind. Fred is too distant from the activities of Susan's section to know what is happening. His knowledge of her section is specific to one person, a finance manager, and beyond that he is unaware. Joe hears indirectly of the discontented and demoralized staff in Susan's section, and, consistent with his resigned defensive practice, abdicates responsibility and authority for the problems the staff face. Joe is convinced he cannot do anything about it (a rationalization). This, of course, only further frustrates Susan's staff, and turnover is becoming a problem. Once again, the psychologically defensive workplace produces paradoxical, unacknowledged, or, at the minimum, hard-to-resolve interpersonal conflict and, as a result, compromised organizational performance.

Joe and Melanie

Melanie is in charge of a product line. She is untrusting, arrogant, controlling, judgmental, can be exceptionally punitive (the arrogant–vindictive psychologically defensive practice), and is mistrusted and disliked by her staff, who see her as incompetent. Melanie has a long history with the organization, including a transfer from Allen's section, where she had been the manager. This transfer, initiated several years ago by Fred to make way for Allen, was viewed as a demotion by Melanie. Since then, Melanie has had numerous angry outbursts at her staff—tantrums during which she humiliated and denigrated them in public. Melanie has to have her way, regardless of what her staff tell her. Fred is aware of these outbursts and understands that there is a morale problem. However, he does not wish to confront the problem and, like Joe, he finds it relatively easy to ignore the situation, since she is not working on any of his pet projects. Since Joe does not wish to deal with it either, Melanie's arrogant and vindictive behavior has no limits placed on it and her staff hate it.

In sum, Joe's resigned psychologically defensive practice combines with Fred's arrogant–vindictive psychologically defensive practice and the perfectionistic, narcissistic, and arrogant–vindictive practices of his immediate subordinates to create a psychologically defensive workplace that leads to gridlock in terms of seeking better organizational performance. In addition, Joe's role and defensive practices are understood to not necessarily be of his own choosing and, therefore, organization dysfunction cannot necessarily be changed by terminating Joe.

ROLE PERFORMANCE AND THE PSYCHOLOGICALLY DEFENSIVE PRACTICES: A RETROSPECTIVE

This chapter has thus far used the theoretical perspective of role behavior as a means of understanding how the psychologically defensive practices influence interpersonal relationships and contribute to the development of the psychologically defensive workplace. The case illuminated the many ways that these psychologically defensive practices can be used to better understand paradoxical, unacknowledged, undiscussable, and dysfunctional behavior that everyone experiences and observes in the workplace. The following section is provided to further explore the theoretical nature of the connection between the psychologically defensive practices and the interpersonal world at work. The psychologically defensive practices are discussed from the point of view that they are acted out by managers and executives.

The Perfectionistic Psychologically Defensive Practice

The perfectionistic psychologically defensive practice leads to the distinctive interpersonal behavior described in Figure 3.2 (as do all of the psychologically defensive practices discussed). The perfectionist feels superior to others as a result of establishing demanding performance criteria few can meet and, if they are met, there are always higher criteria that can be set ("Yes, I can see you finally did it, but . . ."). When the perfectionist becomes anxious, others become the focus of unrelenting, harsh, and highly judgmental criticism even if they are not doing anything particularly different than in the past. Their working relationship with the perfectionist is, therefore, unpredictable and seldom rewarding. They may, however, during the process of exhausting themselves in trying to meet the perfectionist's standards, accomplish a lot of good work and very likely come to feel better (more perfect) than others who do not work for their boss. This often results in a chauvinistic esprit de corps, in which their bad self feelings are projected onto others who they feel superior to (just like their boss does to them). It is, therefore, possible to see how the perfectionistic psychologically defensive tendency comes full circle to affect the interpersonal relationships that employees of the perfectionist have with others. Also to be appreciated is that, given time, a process of employees selecting in and out of working with a perfectionistic boss results in the development of a relatively homogeneous work group which, in some ways, enjoys suffering under the punishing direction of their perfectionistic boss while also feeling superior to everyone else. This leads to the development of perfectionistic groups and organizational cultures discussed in Chapters 4 and 5.

The Arrogant–Vindictive Psychologically Defensive Practice

The arrogant–vindictive psychologically defensive practice also leads to the distinctive interpersonal behavior. The arrogant–vindictive individual feels superior to others but is also openly contemptuous and feels that he or she has nothing to lose by being demanding and aggressive. This individual does not see him- or herself as particularly likable and has essentially abandoned the possibility, thereby unleashing unlikable behavior without social sanctions being present. As a result, others become the focus of paranoid suspicions (it is felt that they may be trying to take advantage of or replace this individual), and open contempt is displayed for their skills, performance, and them as individuals who possess their own thoughts, feelings, and aspirations. Nobody is as good as the arrogant–vindictive personality, and he or she is here to prove it every day by beating down all opposing points of view. Those who are foolish enough to voice different opinions can expect to be subjected to an unrelenting interpersonal attack that might have few limits placed upon it by the individual or the organization. The offending and, therefore, targeted person is "bad" and everyone is told that this is unequivocally true, thereby laying the foundation for unlimited open aggression and undermining without any sense of conscience. The "badness" makes any means of punishment and destruction appropriate. Working relationships with the arrogant–vindictive person are, therefore, filled with uncertainty as to what will come next (fear and management by intimidation). Those who stay may identify with their aggressor and, in so doing, become aggressors themselves. They may, in a sense, feel that they are better and tougher than everyone else and, if anyone doubts this, they are also ready to prove it. They must win as a group, no matter what. Once again, it must be appreciated that, given time, a process of employees selecting in and out of working with their arrogant–vindictive boss results in the development of a relatively homogeneous work group which enjoys inflicting suffering upon others who are foolish enough to question their arrogance. A group and organizational culture of paranoia, arrogance, and vindictive behavior results.

The Narcissistic Psychologically Defensive Practice

The narcisstic psychologically defensive practice results in the person wanting to be admired by unquestioningly loyal others who are prepared to "suck up" to this great individual who has the big ideas. In return, they are rewarded with personal approval, favors, and possibly promotion and organizational resources. Those who do not are labeled as bad and rejected by the narcissist and possibly, at his or her direction, the group or organization. When the narcissist becomes anxious, others have to immediately and even profusely respond by making the individual feel less anxious and better about him- or herself. Many compliments may be rendered as recollections of past glories. It is tacitly understood that everyone is expected to accept responsibility for all problems while passing all the glory to this individual. Anyone who serves as a messenger of bad news is expected to be unceremoniously killed off. Everyone is, in a sense, used and sucked dry of good self feelings while being held responsible for all negative events which may lead to disposal through scapegoating and termination. These employees, in return for their suffering, come to treat others in the same way as their superior treats them. Their subordinates and others in the organization are expected to provide them with stores of good self feelings, admiration, and approval, while sheltering them from bad news. Once again, it is possible to see how this psychologically defensive practice comes full circle to affect the interpersonal relationships that employees have with others. And, once again, it is apparent how narcissistic group and organizational cultures can emerge and dominate work and organizational performance.

A NOTE ON SPLITTING AND PROJECTION AND THE CREATION OF BAD OBJECTS

In each of the above psychologically defensive practices, others are eventually aggressed in some way only after they are first identified as being bad. As noted, being bad enables the use of punishing and destructive interpersonal behavior without the threat of social sanction. After all, the person is bad. Others, it may be felt, are imperfect, feared as trying to take over, or unadmiring and unapproving. The perfectionist locates imperfection in others, thereby securing perfection for him- or herself. Dynamics such as this are frequently used such as the depiction of the Japanese during World War II as blood thirsty ogres that needed killing (not unlike the gooks, commies, slopes, cong, or arabs, any of whom might be "bombed back into the stone age").

Splitting and projection enables individuals and even an entire nation to split off their bad feelings about themselves and locate these feelings in an enemy which may then be righteously killed. The split between good and bad is clear, powerful, and unquestioned. Of course, in reality the split does not exist, as everyone has both good and bad parts. What is important to appreciate in this type of dynamic is that the emergence of an unquestionably all-bad other (an enemy) should be one of the first things to attract one's attention to the fact that psychologically defensive splitting and projection are involved.

The Self-Effacing Psychologically Defensive Practice

The self-effacing psychologically defensive practice results in an executive or employee who is simply not able to be in control of anything and, therefore, relies upon others to take charge. In return for being able to assume the desired role of dependence, this individual is unwaveringly loyal and supportive as long as his or her dependency needs are met and the person feels liked (even loved) and taken care of. When this individual becomes anxious, others become the focus of unrelenting pressure to take charge, even if a catastrophe threatens and no one appears to be ready to take charge. In any group of employees there eventually arises an individual who is sufficiently anxious about what is happening to venture onto the thin ice of taking personal responsibility for and leading an effort to respond to a crisis. In return, the self-effacing superior or employees in the group gladly follow. However, in the event of failure no one will be there to back up the possibly maimed leader, as it is still his or her tacit role to take care of self-effacing followers.

It is again easy to see how a homogeneous group may develop around a self-effacing leader or employee group. Those who remain in the group are often willing to step in to take charge to take care of the self-effacing leader. They also know that if they fail no one will be there to bail them out and, as a result, they too may feel that they need to be dependent and taken care of from time to time, thereby promoting take-charge behavior by others in the group. It should also be appreciated that interpersonal rivalry may develop among those who see taking charge as an opportunity to advance their interests and careers.

The Resigned Psychologically Defensive Practice

The resigned psychologically defensive practice is the result of a leader or employee who is not comfortable either acting masterfully and taking charge or being helpless and letting others take change. Both kinds of behavior are rejected, leaving only one solution: giving up and withdrawing from active participation in organizational life. The leader (or employee) becomes more than merely remote—he or she becomes unavailable. Those who work for or with this individual feel abandoned during stressful times, when the defensive practice is most likely to be acted out. The leadership vacuum must be filled by someone and usually is by those who feel anxious about events. Taking charge is less threatening than suffering through the aversive event. However, unlike under the self-effacing superior, those who take charge from the resigned superior may be resented, discouraged, or even attacked for creating unnecessary problems and anxiety. It may be argued that if no one does anything the problem will go away. This discourages volunteer leadership and may result in a group, department, or organization that is both leaderless and unable to locate anyone willing to lead. Everyone seems to be disconnected from reality, having entered into a timeless state where they are waiting for the "hammer to fall." Anyone offering direction from without is also rejected, including interventions from the top of the organization. Everyone is afraid or unable to act. Once again, a clear pattern of interpersonal relationships is observed to be created by the psychologically defensive practice (no one is supposed to do anything), which can lead to both group and organizational cultures of avoidance.

SUMMARY

What has been learned about roles in organizations? First, despite organizational structure and procedures, roles are ultimately formulated and interpreted by those who fill them. This means that understanding character structure in the form of the psychologically defensive practices is essential to a more holistic and systematic understanding of workplace roles. Second, roles are not performed in isolation. Key roles, such as Joe's, are augmented by the roles others have in the organizational system. In this case, it can be stated with some certainty that roles (and, therefore, organizational norms, decisions, strategies, and actions) in the psychologically defensive workplace are determined by unconscious interpersonal dynamics driven by the psychologically defensive practices. The significance of this interdependency is further discussed in Chapter 8.

THE PSYCHOLOGICALLY DEFENSIVE SIDE OF GROUP DYNAMICS

5

The Mob Within

> Mobs in their emotions are much like children, subject to the same tantrums and fits of fury.
>
> Euripides, *Orestes*, 408 B.C.

> In the hands of vicious men, a mob will do anything. But under good leaders it's quite a different story.
>
> Euripides, *Orestes*, 408 B.C.

Beneath the surface of every work group is a mob. Freud's (1922) *Group Psychology and the Analysis of the Ego* intimates this verdict, a psychological truth often ignored by contemporary management thinkers and practitioners in their romance with the team and work-group culture. In the shadow of every committee and staff meeting lurks the unconscious desires and aggressive feelings of executives and employees.

The workplace is filled with many types of groups, ranging from highly formalized groups, such as the governing board, to informal groups formed spontaneously among employees with an indeterminate span of existence (a Friday-night bowling team). Members of organizations are simultaneous members of many different workplace groups that have many different purposes. All of this diversity can easily encourage the belief that there are few underlying variables that are common to all groups. This assumption, however, is not true. Groups, because they are composed of people, all of whom have occasion to act out their psychologically defensive practices, share in common much more than might initially be expected.

Locating and exploring these underlying psychologically defensive similarities, which usually exist out of awareness but can dominate group members and, by extension, group dynamics, is the key to understanding groups in the psychologically defensive workplace (Bion 1961). Groups invariably contain the latent potential of an irrational, psychologically defensive mob beneath the often soothing and anxiety-reducing aspects of their apparent orderly existence and dependable daily performance. The irrational and psychologically defensive elements of the mob within are especially likely to surface during times of stressful organizational change, such as leadership transitions, downsizings, rapid expansions or mergers, budgetary revisions, and audits. When anxieties run high over fear of loss of control and predictability, the psychologically defensive practices emerge in full force. As a result, many complex, psychologically defensive, and, therefore, hard-to-understand individual, interpersonal, and group dynamics begin to dominate the workplace and create dysfunction.

The spontaneous and unconscious aspects of how group members feel in response to their anxiety, their group leader, and the group and its actions often result in a convergence of their psychologically defensive practices. This out-of-awareness but interactive process of convergence (unconscious collusion) serves eventually to govern thoughts, feelings, and actions and produce three psychologically defensive group cultures: homogenized, institutionalized, and autocratic (Allcorn 1989b; Diamond and Allcorn 1987). Fully understanding the emergence of these psychologically defensive group cultures is directly linked to the psychologically defensive practices but, in the case of group dynamics, these practices are recast as three unconscious appeals: to mastery (perfection, arrogance and vindictiveness, and narcissism), to love (dependence), and to freedom (withdrawal). These appeals form the underlying psychologically defensive nature of group members' relationships to each other, their leader, and the group (Allcorn 1988; Horney 1950).

EXPLORING THE PSYCHOLOGICALLY DEFENSIVE APPEALS

The appeals of mastery, love, and freedom have their origins in what children internalize as a result of their identification with parents, who are society's agents of enculturation. Enculturation introduces expectations of others and frustrated desires and needs. The child naturally responds with ever-greater levels of interpersonal anxiety. The anxiety, in turn, leads children to rely upon the psychologically defensive appeals to protect themselves against their anxiety. The appeal to which they come to depend upon most shapes their personality as well as their life and their goals. The psychologically defensive appeals may, therefore, be understood to shape character.

In the psychologically defensive workplace, the appeals to mastery, love, and freedom become the unconscious, unifying, and undiscussable psychologically defensive themes or sentiences of the three psychologically defensive group cultures. These themes describe the subjective and intersubjective emotional content of group life during stressful times. This emotional content is discovered by examining workplace relationships and, in particular, the leader–follower dyad, which invariably becomes the container for many unconscious group dynamics. Leaders and followers create an intersubjective space filled with thoughts, feelings, and actions that are the experience of group life and its meaning for leader and follower. This unique, unconscious, but symbolically rich mixture of potentials or valences is what may be observed in action and, therefore, documented, understood, and diagnosed relative to the three psychologically defensive group cultures. In sum, the response of leaders and group members to workplace anxieties are symbolized by a particular psychologically defensive appeal and the associated psychologically defensive group culture.

Understanding the typology of psychologically defensive group cultures (homogenized, institutional, and autocratic) and their underlying appeals (mastery, love, and freedom) enables one to develop insight into the psychologically defensive dynamics that govern group behavior (the mob within). Of course, it must be noted that there are many times, if not much of the time, when work groups are not filled with these psychologically defensive appeals and group cultures. This nondefensive work group, the intentional work group, is able to learn from experience because it contains psychologically defensive group dynamics, thereby providing the basis for more reflective and authentic performance during times of stressful organizational events and change.

In sum, the psychologically defensive appeals and matching group cultures provide a unique and theoretically rich window from which to view, participate in, and manage group dynamics. However, before continuing to explore this theoretical perspective of group life, several important provisos must be mentioned.

Proviso One

It must be appreciated that the psychologically defensive appeals and group cultures can and do change, even during a one-hour meeting. They are dynamic. A meeting may start with a despondent and dependent group culture in which feeling victimized, helpless, and dependent is the overwhelming group sentience. However, ideas may be generated during the meeting that offer hope of group salvation, and members may gradually come to feel angry and even paranoid that they are being attacked by a senior-level executive. They may leave the meeting committed to fighting back and perhaps winning at any cost. In sum, although the following discussion describes types of psychologically defensive appeals and group cultures, they exist in a dynamic, larger context where rapid and frequent changes do occur (Allcorn 1989b). Discussing all of these possibilities could fill many volumes and will not be undertaken here in favor of thoroughly explaining the types of psychologically defensive group cultures and the dynamics within and between them.

Proviso Two

Groups may contain, over a long period of time, one psychologically defensive appeal and group culture that has worked well to contain member anxiety. Changing this culture can be extraordinarily frustrating, as the group is comfortable with it and, indeed, dependent upon it to contain anxiety. As a result, the group and leader are exceedingly resistant to change unless they experience sufficient anxiety that calls into question the adequacy of their collective compromise and reaction formations. This is illustrated by the following case example.

For twenty years, a large university has been run by a president who is the consummate micromanaging master autocrat. Under his omnipresent watchful eye, the university grew and prospered. In fact, it grew so large and complex that highly centralized, top-down management was perceived by the governing board to be introducing dysfunction into university operations. The president was eventually encouraged to step down by the governing board and a new, laissez-faire president was hired.

The new president immediately announced a policy of decentralizing power and responsibility. Every school was to become a "tub on its own bottom," and every Dean responsible for balancing his or her books. However, all key administrative employees, information systems, and all aspects of the organizational structure were designed by the past president to feed him control, information, and power. Replacing the president and announcing the new policy was essentially done in a vacuum in which the implications of implementing the proposed changes were not considered. Those in control of the management and information systems continued to maintain control, which had the effect of limiting the amount of information and control Deans and department chairs could exert in their now vastly more-empowered roles.

Similarly, many organizational aspects of the university were separated from each other (finance, information, operations, facilities). They had been entirely coordinated by the past president. Horizontal communication (personal or electronic) and working relationships were simply not needed to any great extent. Coordination began to break down because the new president did not assume the role of master coordinator. This resulted in the centralized groups of university administrators relying more and more upon an institutionalized approach to accomplishing their work. They felt that they had to maintain control, protect their turf, and avoid acknowledging that their new role was not to control but rather to support the Deans in their work. This resulted in slow, painstaking, and often contentious negotiations around all aspects of change and work. When this very slow process threatened the survival of several schools, there arose a wish within the schools to be separate and left alone to do their work, uninhibited by the complex, bureaucratic systems of the university. Eventually, the academic medical center was legally separated from the university, in part because of the inability of the university's rigid, control-oriented, fragmented, and bureaucratic systems to support rapid change in the health-care delivery industry which the center had to respond to. This case example illustrates the first proviso and the autocratic, institutionalized, and homogenized psychologically defensive group cultures to be discussed in this chapter.

It must also be appreciated that groups can contain more than one psychologically defensive culture at a time, even though one may predominate at any given moment. Often there are subgroups of individuals (even one person) who identify with other psychologically defensive group cultures and speak to them when a propitious moment seems to exist. This effort may then lead the group to this new culture. As a result, groups in the workplace may vacillate between the three types of psychologically defensive group cultures. Dependent group members may seek a powerful autocratic leader who will take charge and save them from their problems and anxieties, while also wishing to make sure that their leader and everyone else is under control or that their freedom and autonomy is assured. These provisos must be noted and remembered in order to appreciate the true complexity revealed by the following discussion.

THE APPEAL TO MASTERY

The appeal to mastery, despite its adaptiveness to many situations, is, nonetheless, a compulsive appeal that has as its aim removing or controlling the experience of anxiety. The leader and group members believe that, by an outpouring of highly mobilized and almost limitless energy, they can gain control over virtually any situation. It is felt that anything can be accomplished. The appeal, as noted, arises from and authorizes the three psychologically defensive practices: perfectionist, arrogant–vindictive, and narcissistic.

This appeal, therefore, involves exciting expansive feelings. Members of an athletic team may think of themselves and their team as indomitable and others as imperfect, inferior, and worthy of defeat. The leader of a department may make it clear to everyone in the organization that his or her department and its members are better than other departments and their employees. When carried to an extreme, the appeal to mastery results in the development of a reckless, indifferent, and even perverse chauvinism toward others, in which they are looked down upon and may be uncompromisingly criticized and aggressed in the belief that there will be no social sanction ("They deserve what they get"). It should be noted that the psychologically defensive dynamic of identification with the role of aggressor (the group leader) contributes to the explanation of these group dynamics. At the same time, the group and its leaders feel worthy of being admired, respected, and approved of; after all, in their minds they are taking charge to make sure work goes well.

This psychologically defensive occurrence is facilitated by splitting and projection. Feelings of weakness, helplessness, worthlessness, and dependency are detested by the leader and group and are, therefore, located in others (leaving the group feeling the opposite—powerful and in control), who then become the target of their criticism and aggression. The group may constantly criticize the work of others and openly aggress those who question what they are doing, while also feeling that they deserve to be admired and provided more power to "get things back on track."

The appeal to mastery is illustrated by the turn-around specialist, who is hired in from the outside to transform an organization into a "lean, mean fighting machine" that is highly competitive and profitable. These individuals and the groups that they form around them (often outsiders or consultants) must feel that they can gain control of the organization, its employees, and its problems or they would not feel that they could do the job placed before them by the governing board. However, the job is filled with threat and anxiety, which provokes the psychological defensive practice of mastery and the concomitant culture in the leadership group.

The development of a mastery-based work-group culture leads to rapid downsizing, restructuring, and work redesign, with little attention paid to the impacts of these changes upon the employees and morale. These radical and often destructive methods, it is argued by the new leader and his or her followers, are sanctioned by the great threat of failure facing the organization. In fact, it is often believed that past management and the current employees are at fault for running the organization into the ground, and that they deserve what they get. Resistance is readily addressed by outplacement.

Everyone and everything is subjected to searing, detailed, and unrelenting criticism, without regard to their adaptive aspects. Everything is unacceptable. Everything must be changed. The turn-around leader and his or her support group cannot, at any time, question themselves as to whether they are doing the right thing (group think). Their decisions and actions cannot be questioned by others without the risk of exclusion from participation and possible termination. Equally important is avoidance of acknowledging that the changes are often abruptly implemented in a top-down fashion with little or no explanation or participation on the part of management or employees. Organizational morale begins to plummet along with trust in top management. Free-floating anxiety abounds, as everyone comes to know that they may ultimately be sacrificed on the crucible of downsizing, restructuring, and work redesign. This anxiety comes full circle to create a self-fulfilling outcome—the further evolution of the group culture, around this leader, toward mastery. Everyone who has any doubt is excluded from the group. The leader must assemble a winning team that can dominate the organization, its members, and, by extension, their own anxiety. The ultimate evolution of the mastery-oriented group culture is that the goals of the leader must be zealously followed without question. Group members become a highly disciplined and elite team of "shock troops," who carry out the will of their leader without question or conscience.

THE APPEAL TO LOVE

The use of the word love in the rational, impersonal, and professional workplace may seem to be a paradox. However, everyone silently hopes to be taken care of by another or others who effortlessly meet every need. This group's leader and members act as though they expect to have their security and self-esteem needs magically met. Leaders who appeal to love do not feel that they are capable of mastering others and the work of the organization and may, in fact, abhor overt dominating and controlling behavior, which they compulsively avoid. As a result they act out a role of passiveness and dependency and are prepared to wait for someone else to step forward to take charge, someone who they can support. Others in the group or the organization may step forward to fill the leadership void when the anxiety over inaction becomes too great for them to tolerate. However, when the members of the group also predominantly assume a role of dependency (often encouraged by this leader and many group members), the group develops a culture of dependency where no one within the group feels as though he or she is able or willing to act decisively and risk being criticized, ostracized, and rejected for becoming countercultural. As a result, others are constantly looked to for help. A losing team may feel that it would take a miracle, an act of God, or the location of a superstar to win. A department, even if given clear instructions, may balk at acting upon them, preferring rather to be led by the person who gave the instructions. In sum, psychologically defensive, love-oriented work-group culture results in a group leader and members who prefer to let others run the show while hoping that they will be taken care of in return for their caring and devoted support and loyalty.

The appeal to love is usually compatible with the presence of a master autocrat who expects to make all the decisions (the appeal to mastery). This results in the selection of others who see him or her as being in control and themselves as relatively helpless and dependent. The autocrat, however, is more than willing to try to take care of everyone and everything in return for unquestioning, devoted loyalty. Anyone who is presumptuous enough to question his or her powerful boss is quickly put down, if not surreptitiously removed. All group members are expected to consistently yield to the autocrat and his or her immediate subordinates (in-group). At an extreme, no one and nothing moves without permission. Those who seek roles of caretaking codependency, in which the autocrat makes all of the decisions, appear to have their every need met while being able to split off and project their undesirable mastery-oriented impulses onto their group leader (who welcomes them). They become helpless and morbidly dependent and accept considerable abuse from the autocrat, who views them with arrogant contempt and feels free to be vindictively abusive and critical. This example illustrates the connection between the two types of psychologically defensive appeals. They are compatible with each other and create the illusion of a workable group dynamic.

THE APPEAL TO FREEDOM

Freedom is also a word that is not often mentioned at work. However, everyone may hope, from time to time, to simply be left alone, especially when the going gets tough. Avoiding others and problems, it is felt, leads to less stress and anxiety, but at the cost of losing one's zest for living and ability or willingness to cope with the many problems that work life offers. The leader and the group's members hold few goals and aspirations which they feel will require taking the risks that inevitably accompany personal growth and development as well as accomplishing work. Rather than face the accompanying anxiety, they prefer to be left alone, both as individuals and as a group. The world shrinks to oneself and one's group, and outsiders are felt to be threatening. The result is atomization in the form of severe group and organizational fragmentation, in which everyone becomes detached, indifferent, and separate. Anyone who emerges to try to take charge is ignored and limited by group members and may even be actively sanctioned ("We don't do that sort of thing here"). Active participation in work life is avoided in favor of shutting out the world to gain an inner individual and group peace, not unlike a cult or monastery that abandons, as near as possible, connection to the world. Similarly, departments in a large organization can be observed to have become almost completely disconnected from the larger organization and those the department is supposed to serve. Everyone in the department becomes preoccupied with being left alone in order to avoid coercive external influences, such as meeting an individual or group goal set by management or responding to customer or client complaints. As a result, the group may act as though it has entered a timeless state of independent existence, where aversive influences from the larger organization are avoided.

The appeal to freedom may be observed to exist in a variety of different types of groups, but may not appear unless the group is pressed to take action and made to feel anxious. A group that is under attack by top management in the form of downsizing, restructuring, and work redesign may want to avoid the resulting coercive and punishing influences rather than embrace them and contribute to the change. The group's leader and its members may constantly withdraw from participation and become ever more resistant to taking direction.

Within the group the threat of being downsized makes everyone exceedingly anxious about his or her job. This encourages greater emotional retreat from organizational events and from each other. Employees become progressively more worried about themselves, their families and their careers, and they emotionally disengage to control their anxiety. In sum, the search for freedom and anxiety-free peace and quiet within organizations is exceptionally seductive during stressful times. This appeal and the appeals to mastery and love are generally incompatible, as this appeal discourages being dominated and controlled or taking care of others by taking charge.

THE APPEALS IN RETROSPECT

At first glance, the appeals to mastery, love, and freedom may seem to have some virtue. Certainly, as independent values they may be viewed positively. The executive driven by the appeal to freedom may prove to be sensitive to his or her employees' needs for independence and, in so doing, appear to express to them his or her acknowledgement of their competence and good judgment. The employee driven by the appeal to love may find satisfaction in the experience of working for an all-controlling autocrat or belonging to a large and powerful group or organization. The individual motivated by mastery may be the best source of information, technical talent, and taking charge during stressful times. Yet, when examined from Karen Horney's perspective (1950), the manner in which people compulsively and obsessively pursue these values introduces something rather disturbing into the workplace. Work and organizational artifacts, such as power and authority, take on an entirely new psychologically defensive meaning.

Horney found that individuals who rely upon these appeals for compensatory and defensive reasons often eventually produce dysfunctional, counterproductive, and even destructive outcomes. For Horney, the counterproductive and obsessive–compulsive side of the appeals to mastery, love, and freedom represent psychologically defensive compromise formations that attempt to resolve inner conflicts that have their origins in the flawed parent and child dyad. These flawed relationships produce self-deficits and low self-esteem in adults, who then compensate by rigidly and narrow-mindedly pursuing one of the appeals.

PSYCHOLOGICALLY DEFENSIVE WORK-GROUP CULTURES: THE PSYCHOLOGICALLY DEFENSIVE APPEALS IN ACTION

The three psychologically defensive group cultures provide new insights into understanding group dynamics in organizations. The development of psychologically defensive and homogenous institutional and autocratic group dynamics are understood to be the result of a convergence of psychologically defensive practices that have a common emotional bond or sentience that dominates group life. They also do not ultimately resolve the inner conflicts group members share, because of their compromise and reaction-formation-like responses to stressful organizational events. As a result, each psychologically defensive group culture contains within it the seeds of its own dysfunction (destruction). These paradoxical group dynamics are important to keep in mind as the psychologically defensive work-group cultures are discussed.

The Autocratic Group Culture: The Appeal to Mastery

The appeal to mastery is associated with perfectionism, arrogance, vindictiveness, and narcissism ("I know what is best, do as you are told"). The autocratic group culture relieves member anxiety by promoting the belief among its members that a powerful, often charismatic leader will control everything. The leader, it is hoped, will save everyone from their problems and make them feel good (free from anxiety). As a result, the leader ends up holding most of the power in the group and can promote the correct behavior (as defined by the leader) that, it is hoped, will minimize everyone's anxiety—including that of the leader who fears being attacked by followers and others outside of the group as he or she fulfills his or her vision.

Attack is feared because this leader often acts in ways that are opposed by others (sometimes many others), which tends to create an alienated, disenfranchised out-group within the group which may try to strike back at anytime. At the same time, some individuals come to be known to be the leader's favorites. Those who question the leader can expect to be scapegoated as not being team players and described as problem people who should probably leave the organization. These interpersonal dynamics eventually lead to divisiveness. There are those who are in and those who are out.

Yet another aspect of this group culture is the at times perverse sense of paranoia that the group will be in some way harmed by external events or others. This paranoia is readily turned into mastery-oriented energy to resist, fight back, and overcome the perceived enemy, who is identified and defined by the leader. The enemy that makes group members feel anxious, it is asserted, is outside of the group, which directs group member attention away from reflecting upon group and leadership dynamics and accompanying feelings of being dominated and controlled, and, as a result, alienated and anxious.

The Seeds of Self-Destruction The charismatic leader is also found to be only too human and a person who can exercise poor judgement (often encouraged with growing arrogance, self-importance, and isolation from reality), which is distressing to group members who expect perfect performance and anxiety-free existence. Interpersonal rivalries spawned by access to the leader, and deeply felt desires to receive his or her attention and rewards, also create conflict that disrupts work. These failures and disruptions often lead to the reemergence of anxiety.

If the problems are severe enough, the governing board, management, or group members may eventually come to feel that replacing the leader is necessary. However, it is intuitively understood that this action is filled with the danger of being attacked by the leader and his or her followers. Feelings of fear and guilt may also inhibit change. Loss of the leader reintroduces the fear into the now highly dependent group that their dependency needs will not be met. The more that removal of the leader is contemplated, the greater the fear of uncontrollable anxiety (approach-avoidance anxiety). Feelings of guilt over killing off the leader may also be felt, further adding to the discomfort of making the change. It is at this juncture of increased anxiety and psychological defensiveness that a new leader may emerge to move the group to one of the other types of psychologically defensive group cultures.

Organizations are filled with these types of outcomes. An irritable, unpredictable, and not particularly knowledgeable or effective leader insists upon, nonetheless, making all decisions, perhaps out of fear of being found out and replaced. This leader collects around him or her layers of others who are subservient, but equally controlling. They seek power, like their leader, in order to be admired as well as protected against the intentions of others who differ with them. Anyone who gets in the way is found to be at fault and removed. Scapegoating becomes a major part of the autocratic group culture. The leader, in order to protect him- or herself from being found at fault, readily blames his or her immediate subordinates, who may be turned upon and demoted or fired for operating problems. The client or customer may also be found to be at fault for being too demanding or uncooperative. Competitors and the government may receive the full measure of blame as well. Everyone and everything is at fault except the leader, who feels and even points out that the source of the problem is others who do not unquestionably submit to and follow their leader. This individual feels that if only he or she has sufficient power, everything can be controlled. It should be noted that subordinates will frequently blame and scapegoat each other to maintain blame-free existence, while avoiding confronting the threatening reality that it is their leader who is at fault.

This group culture is all too familiar in the workplace. Providing a case example is hardly needed as this psychologically defensive group culture is frequently relied upon to control workplace anxiety.

The Institutionalized Group Culture: The Appeal to Love

The institutionalized group will follow a leader who promises to create a more structured approach that controls their anxiety. This approach attempts to control anxiety by creating rules, regulations, and formal roles that control

all interpersonal interactions and all aspects of work, including client or customer interface and behavior. Every group member knows exactly what he or
she is supposed to do, what others are supposed to do, and the exact procedures by which work is to be accomplished. Group members willingly follow instructions, even if they are humiliating and limiting, to fulfill their need
to be provided a regulated work setting where their anxieties are allayed ("I
will be as you wish"). A hierarchical structure develops around specialization,
in which even the leader is not threatening, as he or she has to follow the rules
of leadership agreed to by the group. The leader's role is, in effect, routinized
or circumscribed as a result of being carefully and completely controlled by
the rules. The ultimate goal of the institutionalized group is to create impersonal control over what its members think, feel, and do, including the leader.
Rigidly adhered-to protocols, paperwork (forms and formats), rules, regulations, and behavioral patterns in the form of roles offer everyone interpersonal
safety and distance while permitting work to be accomplished.

Institutionalization, therefore, fulfills the psychologically defensive nature
of the appeal to love by providing a regulated and, by extension, predictable,
caretaking, and safe organizational culture. Carefully regulated forms of interpersonal dependence emerge in a complex hierarchical and departmental-
ized scheme of interpersonal interaction. Everyone knows what to expect.
Equality of treatment is an expectation (usually unfulfilled). Everyone's needs
for security are to be met by the impersonal, highly controlled, and controlling "system," in what amounts to an unwritten social contract with group
members to make sure that they do not feel that the workplace has elements
that are out of control and, therefore, containing stress and anxiety.

In effect, the compulsive desire to be taken care of and dependent in return
for self-effacing loyalty and dependency is very nicely fulfilled by the creation
of what amounts to an externalization of their psychologically defensive appeal
in the form of an omnipresent, all-knowing, and caring form of psychologically
defensive organizational culture. All behavior is carefully prescribed, circumscribed, and monitored. When an institutionalized cultural norm is violated,
group members usually have at their disposal lengthy complaint and appeal
mechanisms that discourage any further violations of the norm. The constant
pursuit of the elimination of the unpredictable stressful events and anxiety (a
quest that cannot ultimately be fulfilled by this means and may, therefore, be
thought of as self-defeating behavior) leads to ever-greater regulation and
control. This eventually becomes over-controlling micromanagment of virtually all aspects of work, thereby creating more dysfunction.

The Seeds of Self-Destruction   Even though institutionalized groups accomplish work, it is at the cost of losing creativity, flexibility, and the ability
to learn from experience. Bureaucratic hierarchies are notorious for having
difficulty adjusting to new circumstances. Members are expected to suppress
their desires for autonomy; however, self-interest still continuously emerges

in the form of organizational politics, self-protection, special-interest groups, and power plays that disrupt carefully planned and controlled work plans and processes. This outcome, when combined with a lack of flexibility and poor group learning, often ends up threatening the group's ability to accomplish its task and, by extension its long-term survival. The group may, at this point, reinforce its institutionalized behavior with more rules and regulations to get better control, or it might evolve into another type of psychologically defensive group if a leader is present to lead group members in change.

The Homogenized Group Culture: The Appeal to Freedom

This psychologically defensive group culture is a familiar one in the workplace. The appeal to freedom usually arises when neither of the first two appeals works or when they are unavailable to group members to act out because of psychic conflict which precludes being powerful or dependent. The only recourse is resignation (dropping out, disengagement) from active participation, which involves withdrawal from self, others, and organizational life ("Just leave me alone"). This psychologically defensive group culture arises from desires of group members and their leader for autonomy and independence. Members protect themselves from each other by steadfastly maintaining their personal autonomy. Everyone, it is felt, is equal, and therefore no one is better. No one may be distinguished by a special role or should be more powerful than anyone else. This group culture is symbolized by everyone sitting in a large circle where everyone feels coequal.

The Seeds of Self-Destruction   The homogenized group culture, while being embedded within an identifiable group or organization, acts more like a crowd. An observer of a homogenized group understands that the pursuit of autonomy and personal freedom creates a group that lacks clear purpose and effective leadership. Efforts to lead, either by the designated leader or by others, are not heeded. Homogenized group dynamics eventually discourage anyone from trying to lead the group.

When homogenized group members are placed in a stressful, externally imposed circumstance, they readily feel the lack of connectedness to each other as their compulsive and unquestioned pursuit of personal freedom and autonomy to avoid anxiety emerges. They steadfastly cut themselves off from each other to maintain their independence just when they could benefit the most from feeling together to deal with their anxieties. Group members will feel confused, distressed, disoriented, and neither in nor out of the group. Attachment and abandonment anxiety abound (Allcorn 1992, 1994; Bar-Levav 1988). They are there, but do not feel a part of the group or what is going on. They feel that they can neither engage the group nor separate from it.

Anxiety is further enhanced by the group eventually losing touch with its purpose and connection to its operating environment. It acts as though it has entered into a timeless, unchanging state where nothing needs to be accomplished despite considerable evidence to the contrary. Reality testing becomes severely compromised as each member pursues his or her task of highest priority, that of maintaining personal autonomy and interpersonal safety.

Gradually, group members come to feel angry with the group while also fearing what the group may do to them. The lack of connectedness and followership plunges the group into difficulty accomplishing work on its tasks. Under these circumstances withdrawing physically and psychologically becomes the safest thing to do. Individual members also seek support and safety by pairing with others or by joining small subgroups of three or four individuals (each with their own subculture) to create some sense of security. This outcome results in the creation of a subculture of interpersonal dependency and caretaking behavior (the appeal to love, institutionalization), or one where a group leader is sought out (the appeal to mastery, autocracy). These new psychologically defensive group cultures may emerge at any time as another way the group can manage its anxieties.

In sum, if the group's members feel sufficiently threatened, a change may occur to one of the other types of psychologically defensive group cultures if suitable leadership emerges and there are enough group members, who are in enough distress, to follow the new leader and his or her sentient-based subgroup in making the change.

The Intentional Group Culture: Minimal Psychological Defensiveness

Intentional group cultures, unlike the three psychologically defensive group cultures, are relatively free of excessive anxiety. Membership is not threatening. There is little need for members to develop psychological, interpersonal, and group defenses against anxiety. The thoughts and feelings of individuals are acknowledged and respected. Conflicts are explored for what may be learned from them and worked through to resolution, or at least to a point where they no longer block the group's work. Consensus building works because it is accomplished in an open group dynamic where group members feel that their points of view are being heard. Working in the group is usually experienced as fun as well as challenging. The group, while having a designated leader, often receives leadership volunteered by members who have something to contribute, and their leadership efforts are accepted by others, including the formal leader.

Intentional work groups are, however, constantly threatened by the emergence of the excessive anxiety that is omnipresent in modern-day organizations that must operate in a turbulent world-wide marketplace. Intentional work groups may have their integrity compromised by the emergence of leaders who strongly prefer one of the other three psychologically defensive cultures:

homogenized, institutionalized, or autocratic. Such leadership emerges when sufficient anxiety develops. A group member may vigorously point out that the cause of a problem is the lack of sufficient organization and that rules and regulations are absent or are being disregarded. Another member may point out that the group needs a stronger visionary leader. There may also emerge a trend among some members to attack and disregard the contributions of other members. They may act without regard to direction offered by the group's leaders and those interested in continuing to work on the task. These psychologically defensive group cultures are always present in groups and must be recognized and addressed (not suppressed) in order to heed the point being expressed by the emergence of a sentience group and maintain the intentional work-group culture.

SUMMARY

This chapter has introduced two psychologically informed perspectives for understanding group dynamics. The appeals to mastery, love, and freedom, when they become the dominant sentience of a group, lead the group to the three psychologically defensive group cultures (the mob within). These psychologically defensive group cultures each has an unstable compromise formation at its core that group members hope will contain their anxiety, but, ultimately the culture cannot do so perfectly without introducing new anxiety about the group's distressing experience of the group's culture. Each psychologically defensive group culture, therefore, carries within it the seeds of its own destruction as well as the seeds of a new psychologically defensive group culture. In sum, these cultures are suspended in a dynamic relationship to each other and the larger organizational context in which they exist. Change is inevitable, even if it is only accomplished, for example, by the retirement, promotion, transfer, or departure of a group leader who has led the group in the maintenance of a psychologically defensive culture.

The loss of a leader is threatening. His or her departure often leaves a group and work process in place that is so completely attuned to the culture that subsequent leaders may find it difficult to change. Not only will group members see no need for change, anyone endeavoring to bring about change may have to change policies and procedures, information and communication systems, and financial and internal structures, all of which is costly, time consuming, and made all the more difficult by group members who feel that the systems are just fine; after all, they have done the job for the past five, ten, or twenty years.

However, despite this resistance, poor group performance and threat from the operating environment often lead to changes in the group's leadership. A new leader is frequently charged by top management with changing how the group accomplishes its work and perhaps what work is valued (all too often a reaction formation to the previous type of leadership). The combination of perceived and threatened failure and the presence of a new leader usually creates enough distress that group members become anxious and may readily bolt to another psychologically defensive culture or perhaps a more intentional work-group culture that promises to allay their anxiety about change.

THE PSYCHOLOGICALLY DEFENSIVE SIDE OF ORGANIZATIONAL DYNAMICS   6

The most self-conscious people in the world are its leaders. They may also be the most anxious and insecure. As men of action, leaders face risks and uncertainty, and often display remarkable courage in shouldering grave responsibility. But beneath their fortitude, there often lies an agonizing sense of doubt and a need to justify themselves.

Zaleznik 1966, 1

Culture and leadership, when one examines them closely, are two sides of the same coin, and neither can really be understood by itself. In fact, there is a possibility—underemphasized in leadership research—that the *only thing of real importance that leaders do is to create and manage culture.*

Schein 1985, 2

Organizations, regardless of whether they are small and simple or huge and complex, all in one location or scattered around the world, are composed of smaller constituent parts—individuals, employee relationships, and groups. However, when examined as a whole, organizations have a complexity greater than individual, interpersonal, and group dynamics. They are, to coin an old phrase, "greater than the sum of their parts." In effect, they must contain all of these influences and somehow make them function well enough together to accomplish work and fulfill the task of organizational survival.

However, it must also be appreciated that while an organization transcends its parts, the parts and the organization coexist, which makes understanding organizational dynamics extraordinarily difficult. Also to be appreciated is that the psychologically defensive practices of individuals and group cultures coexist in the interactive context of the organization. It is within this larger context that they create a vast network of psychologically defensive dynamics that have an active role in the creation and maintenance of enduring ways of organizing people and work that minimize participant anxiety. These time-tested, familiar, and usually unacknowledged patterns of relating, knowing the organization, and performing work constitute the culture of an organization.

The complex and all-inclusive nature of the organization also squarely introduces the existence of powerful, unconscious, mutually interactive leader/follower dynamics that, in part, determine the leader's self-conception as well as his or her conception of followers and their conception of themselves. These usually unconscious interpersonal dynamics are omnipresent and have a major influence upon leader/follower relations as well as how the culture of the organization is formed and operates in practice. The psychologically defensive practices of an organization's leader and leadership group dominate the entire organization down to the lowest worker. These executives possess much greater power and influence to control people and work than leaders of groups and, as a result, they are a dominant influence on the development and evolution of organizational culture

In sum, organizations, when examined as a whole, represent the overall context or culture in which their employees must function. Every organizational culture contains psychologically defensive elements that serve to protect its CEO, executives, managers, supervisors, and employees from anxieties arising from working together and the ever present necessity to insure that their organization survives in a competitive world. We therefore return to the notion of regulating and controlling the anxiety of executives and employees, anxiety that arises from how the organization works (internal anxiety) and how effective it is at making its way in the evolutionary process of survival in an ever changing marketplace (external anxiety) (Schein 1985). Anxiety and psychological defensiveness become the common threads that tie together individual, interpersonal, and group dynamics within a larger organizational context in which powerful leaders dominate work life.

THE NATURE OF ORGANIZATIONAL CULTURE

Organizational culture may be thought of as existing at four levels: one that is concrete, one that is cognitive and that people are aware of, one that is affective and that people feel, and one that is unconscious and that people are not aware of. The concrete aspects of culture include, literally, the concrete, bricks, mortar, and architecture that create the organization's physical space. Also included are such things as organizational artifacts: logos, letterhead, communication systems, polices and procedures, and standard protocols—anything that can be pointed to.

The cognitive aspects of culture include such things as ways of thinking about the organization, its task environment, its work, and how employees relate to each other. Also included are aspects of work that must be learned, such as how meetings should be conducted, social formalities, rituals, myths, espoused philosophies, mission statements and goals, and how the organization is structured (Schein 1990). These are ways of learning about and knowing how to think and act to be consistent with organizational norms and ideals. They are the often taken for granted, predictable, and anxiety-reducing aspects of what the organization seems like to its members. However, it must also be acknowledged that they limit other ways of thinking and acting, which may paradoxically limit innovation and create operating problems that promote anxiety.

The affective aspects of an organization and its culture are how it feels to be a part of the organization. Organizations can encourage their members to feel like secure and valued contributors, an impersonal human resource, or a cost to be managed. Members can feel excited and challenged about their work and working with each other, or anxious, alienated, threatened, depressed, and angry (feelings which seem to abound in large-scale contemporary organizations). They may feel that they are a part of a great enterprise that is successful, or they may feel that their organization is ineffective and in harm's way. Organizations, their leaders, and their cultures provoke a great many exceptionally strong feelings on the part of their members. Organizational life is never free of how members feel about their work, themselves, and others with whom they work.

The unconscious level of organizational culture can be thought of as the *proto-culture*. It is the precultural elements of the concrete, cognitive, and affective aspects of organizational culture that are, in part, created by and changed in response to the unconscious life of an organization's members and their leaders (Diamond 1993). These elements exist in the unconscious intersubjective nature of individual, interpersonal, group and organizational dynamics created by transference and unconscious psychological defenses, such as the splitting and projection of experience into good and bad to minimize anxiety. These elements of an organization constitute a form of identity—who one is and what or, at the risk of reifying the organization, who it is, in the sense employees seem to know it to exist and have attributes not unlike a person.

These four aspects of organizational culture function together to create a complete experience of work life for members of the organization. Our focus here is upon the unconscious, psychologically defensive elements of organizations and their cultures. This perspective, however, provides new meaning to the other three aspects of organizational life—concrete, cognitive, and affective. This chapter will also explore the roles of leaders and followers in forming and, in return, being formed by the organization.

THE PSYCHOLOGICALLY DEFENSIVE SIDE
OF ORGANIZATIONS AND THEIR CULTURES:
THEIR ORGANIZATIONAL IDENTITY

Organizational identity is the way people unconsciously experience themselves, each other, their work, and their organization. Organizational identity is also a way of conceptualizing the unconscious foundation or deep psychological structure that contributes to the creation of organizations and their cultures (Diamond 1991). In this regard, organizational identity is the unwitting product of the convergence of unconscious coping responses that allay anxiety caused by the stressful aspects of organizational life. It is, therefore, a shared, joint, and intersubjective outcome that arises out of interaction with others. People unconsciously create it.

Organizational identity is acted out in the repetitive, often unacknowledged, but learned ritualistic patterns of behavior and deeply felt emotional workplace attachments (or perhaps today, detachments). These familiar anxiety-allaying patterns of behavior and attachment must, therefore, be understood to be filled with deep unconscious personal meaning that organizes how organizational life is perceived in the hearts and minds of employees.

The psychological nature of this unconscious meaning and experience is created by the development of shared intersubjective structures of self–object relationships, in which one's internal images of work life are created and manipulated in fantasy to help manage the anxieties that arise from the interpersonal workplace (Kohut 1977). These fantasies that create meaning and self-experience are, however, interactive with one's behavior and attachment to others, thereby enabling the process of convergence. These intrapsychic and interpersonal events become, in effect, the mutually shared basis for making daily life comforting, and give meaning to the concrete, cognitive, and affective aspects of work life. They are the first line of defense against the ravages of anxiety created by the uncertain demands of an ever-changing organizational landscape.

Organizational identity can, therefore, be understood to be a psychologically defensive solution to anxiety that includes the use of common psychological defenses, such as splitting and projection, projective identification, and transference, that are acted out in the form of the psychologically defensive practices. These unconscious, psychologically defensive elements of organizational identity can be further explored by revisiting the psychologically defensive appeals to mastery, love, and freedom. These defensive appeals and their accompanying organizational cultures provide a basis for understanding psychologically defensive organizational dynamics, culture, and leadership.

The Psychologically Defensive Appeal to Mastery: The Autocratic Organizational Culture

The appeal to mastery and its component parts, perfectionism, arrogance and vindictiveness, and narcissism, are frequent adaptive responses to uncertainty, loss of control and anxiety in western organizations. Getting control, being in charge, overcoming great odds, and winning are, in many ways, the bedrock of American society. These values are also understood to be the basis for organizational success. Therefore, one expects to find the psychologically defensive appeal to mastery to be highly mobilized in modern-day organizations and leaders, who must compete to survive.

Organizations are all too frequently dominated by their leaders, who see fit to try to manage all aspects of their organization as indicated by their approval of all major and even minor decisions and detailed reviews of all budgets. This top-down organizational culture can be found everywhere and it is likely that all workers have encountered it at some time. The people at the top are powerful, like it like that, and consistently act to conserve their power by making sure no one else has sufficient power or information to offer a threat. All rivals are vanquished in win or lose dynamics in which only the CEO and top management can win. These organizational cultures are tightly controlled, and the appearance of the CEO in work areas often strikes terror into the hearts and minds of employees. These executives feel that it is more important to be feared than liked although admiration is highly sought after and is usually acquired from a cadre of obsequious followers who are hand picked and personally castrated by the CEO to insure their unquestioning loyalty and willingness to follow every order.

Business journals and newspapers are full of reports of winners and losers and frequently ruthless but short-term financially successful behavior. It is also fair to say that those who lead organizations, as well as their members, are anxious about being successful. Anxiety about failure or losing abounds and results in organizations seeking out leaders who promise that they can successfully compete by developing organizational cultures where everyone is highly mobilized to meet the next goal to insure survival. In fact, it is very likely that many of those who are at the top of organizations (or those striving to displace those at the top) experience considerable anxiety and rely upon mastery as a coping mechanism to such an extent that this psychologically defensive appeal essentially takes over most aspects of their personality and, for all practical purposes, becomes their character. These individuals are driven to succeed and will sacrifice their reputation, health, and family to be a winner. Certainly, anything is possible, as documented by such infamous business personalities as Michael Milliken, Ivan Boesky, the many executives involved in the savings and loan bail-out scandal, and even a President such as Richard Nixon. These individuals feel that there should be few limits placed upon them as to what they can do.

CEOs are also often quick to create a defensible perimeter between themselves, the often ruthless actions such as downsizing, and the members of their organization. They are particularly prone to making scapegoating others a fine-tuned pastime, and seldom find themselves to be at fault. Others and events are invariably blamed, and a few colleagues may be sacrificed from time to time. An employee of one organization led by such an individual commented, when asked what it was like to work in the organization, "You never want to go too far out on a limb to try something new—if you get into difficulty, when you turn around no one will be there to back you up." In fact, the CEO in this particular organization was more than willing to saw off the limb behind those who tried new ways of working if the difficulties associated with the change attracted too much negative attention. Scapegoating is highly consistent with the psychologically defensive appeal to mastery. Scapegoats are readily created by perfectionistic criticism, and a list of candidates (a hit list) is readily developed by these CEOs, who remember those who have offended their delicate pride or failed to support narcissist needs. The same employee volunteered, "Once you get on the list, you are on there for life."

At the same time, these CEOs are prone to collect around themselves a layer or two or three of executives who are beholden to the CEO for their jobs and are willing to play along with being controlled and occasionally scapegoated by the CEO. These individuals share many characteristics in common and are much more alike that different (Allcorn 1990). The unconscious contract between these sycophants and their leader is that they must fulfill their narcissistic leader's needs for power, glory, admiration, attention, and unquestioning obedience. They often work hard to make him or her feel good, while also providing a defensible parameter of readily available scapegoats to avoid the necessity of the CEO assuming personal responsibility for actions that promote problems and anxiety. However, the CEO is, of course, more than eager to claim responsibility for successes.

The rather punishing unconscious organizational identity created by such a setting includes many distressing elements that detract from individual, group, and organizational performance. Employees are anxious about accepting the risks of trying new behaviors. They engage in considerable use of psychological defenses, such as denial and rationalization, in order to keep their jobs. The scapegoating of others is anxiously observed without comment. Defensive splitting and projection create an all-powerful CEO and vulnerable and helpless employees who do not envision that they can do anything to defend themselves against the CEO and his or her immediate circle of top managers. All of these shared unconscious dynamics (organizational identity) serve to reinforce the organizational culture of mastery which takes the form of mastery of the employees and organization by the CEO. At the same time, the organization may not be effective and its existence may be threatened. This survival concern further increases the anxiety experienced by the CEO and his or her belief that all he or she needs is more control to solve problems. Scapegoating and the need to feed this CEO narcissistic supplies becomes paramount in order to avoid his or her becoming further fragmented or, conversely, to hold him or her together.

Behaviors such as these are the substance of organizational identity, which promotes the development of a psychologically defensive experience of the workplace and an accompanying culture. Employees unconsciously experience themselves as vulnerable, powerless, not respected, and unable to develop interpersonal boundaries. The unspoken but accepted norms include aversion to risk taking and scapegoating to avoid the assumption of personal responsibility.

The Psychologically Defensive Appeal to Love:
The Institutionalized Organizational Culture

One might think that an organizational identity dominated by unconscious desires to be taken care of in return for servile dependence and loyalty would be incompatible with leadership or, for that matter, an organization's employees. However, an organization that takes care of its people is highly desirable, especially when compared to an organization preoccupied with mastery. This is, therefore, a very common form that organizational culture takes, and it is especially prominent among federal and state departments and agencies. The culture becomes one that is preoccupied with making sure every "i" is dotted and "t" is crossed in order to avoid any possibility of being found to be at fault or held personally accountable. Everyone becomes preoccupied with being defended by rules, regulations, protocol, job descriptions, and grievance procedures. As near as possible, every aspect of work is codified. If taken too far, institutionalization compromises objectivity and the willingness to make tough decisions when the feelings of some employees may be hurt. This organizational culture is comforting to those who enjoy a great deal of anxiety-reducing predictability (being taken care of by the organization). However, it is also experienced as rigid, restrictive, unyielding, and unsupportive by those who seek to explore opportunities to improve performance and advocate change. Very often, these organizations lose their most innovative employees, who invariably look elsewhere for job opportunities that are more fulfilling and permit them opportunities of self-expression in the form to leadership opportunities and getting to try new ways of organizing and performing work (Downs 1967).

A second route by which this type of organization is realized is through the actions of a CEO who, as a result of compulsive tendencies to protect employees from having their feelings hurt, consistently acts to make sure that everyone is treated fairly and, if possible, the same (egalitarianism). How people feel becomes one of the dominant influences of organizational leadership and decision making. In this case, the CEO, in return for being devoted to and caretaking of (loving) employees by regulating the workplace, expects to be loved and taken care of in return.

The quality of intersubjective work life in this caretaking but highly regulated organization is filled with projections of power and competence onto leaders and, more abstractly, the organization who (or which are) are expected to be able to take care of everyone. Employees come to know themselves and each other at an unconscious level as relatively helpless and in need of being taken care of. At the same time, top management is unwittingly cast in the role of having to take care of themselves, each other, the employees, and the organization (something mastery-oriented leaders are willing to do). Leaders, who must face this onerous responsibility, project feelings of incompetence and powerlessness onto the employees, further reinforcing their view that the employees have to be watched every moment and taken care of like little children. This tendency is further promoted by projective identification, in which those in leadership roles are encouraged to feel that they must take care of everyone and everything and that they, in fact, can do so. They, in effect, take in or incorporate the projections of their employees (projective identification), who want to see them as all powerful and able to provide nearly perfect caretaking behavior. This results in unquestioned paternalistic or maternalistic leadership styles and the wish to be taken care of by powerful authority figures.

However, if an organization's leaders are themselves dependent and want to be taken care of, accomplishing work becomes problematic. The focus is on defending everyone's feelings. In this case, either the employees must rise to the occasion or some outside source must provide leadership. In the event that the employees are also dependent, the entire organization is experienced as helpless and in need of rescue, which may take the form of the Board appointing a new CEO, the hiring of consultants, or perhaps the organization may be purchased by another organization that is willing to provide leadership. In any case, the unconscious intersubjective experience of self, others, and the organization is one of helplessness, dependency, and the implicit desire to be taken care of. The resulting culture of the organization and accompanying organizational dynamics are unconsciously invested with this organizational identity that permeates all aspects of the organization and its work, ranging from goal setting, personnel management, supervision, performance evaluation, rules, regulations, policies and procedures, and even employee selection and retention. The organization and how it works, in effect, is dominated by an organizational identity centered around the appeal to love.

The Psychologically Defensive Appeal to Freedom: The Homogenized Organizational Culture

At first glance, this culture may seem to be the least familiar of the three. This organizational culture shares much in common with that of the homogeneous group culture. There exists a paucity of leaders, leadership, connectedness, and interpersonal, intergroup, or interdepartmental cooperation and self-regulation. The various sections of the organization fail to work together effectively and there may even by rivalry. There may literally be "too many bulls in the china shop" or too many stove pipes (vertically organized departments) that defend their turf. These metaphors capture some of the essence of the homogenized organizational culture. The leaders and employees of divisions and departments fail to voluntarily coordinate their work. No one is willing to give up control and everyone pursues a narrowly defined autonomy in which the encroachment of others is avoided at all costs. At the same time, each section wants to make sure that it gets its fair share of the organizational-resource pie.

Working across internal organizational boundaries becomes hazardous and problematic as they are rigorously monitored and defended. Turf battles develop if the encroachment is not ended.

One might then ask what kind of organization this can be. There are, however, many examples. The armed forces of the United States are composed of three main branches—army, navy, and air force. Each pursues its own interests, develops its own goals and objectives, purchases its own equipment according to its own specifications, and competes for a piece of the congressional-funding pie. The invasion of "fortress" Granada revealed the folly of this fragmented approach to organizing the armed forces that so carefully maintained branch autonomy. Each branch competed for a piece of the invasion pie, and when it did occur, to everyone's chagrin, the communications equipment of the three branches was incompatible and a soldier was, at one point, forced to "call home" to the Pentagon via a long distance phone service to pass important invasion information to another branch's personnel.

The recent development of enormous health care delivery networks that combine numbers of hospitals and other health care delivery facilities with many thousands of physicians are confronted with the problem of having evolved a homogeneous organization in which diverse subcultures exist that are intent on maintaining personal, group, or organizational autonomy. Successfully combining them into a super-organization remains a challenge (Allcorn 1995).

The appeal to freedom, as may be observed from these examples, is perhaps the most consistently unadaptive organizational identity. Intersubjective work life is filled with fears of others being controlling or demanding attention. Neither response is felt to be appropriate. Employees attribute malevolent intentions to their supervisors, other parts of the organization, and the organization's senior management. These attributions are supported by projecting their own malevolent, controlling, and needy intentions onto these individuals thereby leaving themselves free of the intentions and, therefore, relatively innocent victims who just want to be left alone. Any effort to supervise, provide direction, or evaluate performance is understood to be a perversely motivated bad influence that must be avoided.

If an entire organization becomes preoccupied with unconsciously fulfilling the appeal to freedom, senior management and employees will also feel that they and their organization are under attack by evil outside forces. They experience themselves, each other, and their organization as good and trying to carry on under adverse circumstances. A corporation may be subjected to a hostile takeover (at least in the minds of the employees) as a result of its own ineffectiveness. However, organization members do not see the problem as their own thereby making the outcome something that they are not responsible for. The leadership and employees of a department of a state government might feel as though their department is always under attack from politicians and its clients and inadequately funded. They just want to be left alone to accomplish their work without constant criticism and attack.

Organizational Identity—In Sum

The notion of organizational identity offers a way of conceptualizing the unconscious psychologically defensive nature of organizational life. It emphasizes that the unconscious lives of employees and leaders form a usually unacknowledged but all pervasive intersubjective network of psychological defensive experience that, in turn, becomes the matrix upon which conscious experience, meaning, and organizational culture evolves. The psychologically defensive appeals, when combined with the notion of organizational identity, offer insights into how organizations get off track and compromise their success and survival. This discussion incorporated the role of leaders in the development of the intersubjective web of organizational life. It is, however, important to more-fully consider the role of leaders in creating psychologically defensive organizations. This will be undertaken from two vantage points: the interaction of organizational leaders with followers and the interaction of followers with organizational leaders.

THE INTERACTION OF LEADERS WITH THEIR FOLLOWERS

CEOs are usually under a lot of pressure to perform and usually feel responsible for the well-being of their organization and, by extension, its employees. This is an onerous weight to bear. Anxiety is, therefore, a common experience, one which promotes severe regression and reliance upon psychological defenses and the psychological defensive practices (Kernberg 1979). The following discussion blends the earlier description of individual, interpersonal, and group psychologically defensive practices with the psychological defenses of splitting and projection, projective identification, and the unconscious context-setting influence that transference has upon leadership dynamics. Before continuing, it is important to remember that thoughts, feelings, and personal attributes can be split-off and projected onto others.

The Shaping of Followers through Executive Projection

Unconscious projection of thoughts, feelings, and personal attributes occurs throughout one's life (Grotstein 1985). Projection leaves a person feeling less anxious because unconscious internal conflict is diminished by separating good from bad experience. The individual experiences self as all good and another individual as all bad, or vice versa. This black and white world of good and bad is simple and comforting. Leaders frequently experience themselves and others in this way.

Projected Thoughts   Leaders must think of themselves as somewhat infallible in order to feel confident that they can direct and control others and the organization. In fact, in many organizations there is an extreme split between what those at the top and the rest of the members of the organization know and think. The metaphor of a human body seems to apply. All the brains are at the top (top management is expected to know) and the rest of the members of the organization become the body, which carries out work as directed, often with the expectation that instructions from the brain will not be questioned. In sum, leaders are expected to be powerful, all knowing, and in charge. Before continuing, it must be again acknowledged that powerful organizational leaders may not necessarily see themselves as fulfilling this role of mastery, and some may act out one of the other two psychologically defensive practices, dependency or withdrawal. The following discussion focuses on mastery as the most common expectation for leaders.

Leaders who want to think of themselves as being in control, knowing everything, achieving perfection in decision making and being worthy of admiration are invested in not thinking of themselves in any other way (although certainly thoughts of dependency and withdrawal exist from time to time). Incompatible thoughts are repressed, suppressed, or disposed of through the psychologically defensive processes of denial, splitting, and projection onto others in the organization who are then experienced as not able to think and control work as well as the leader or leadership group. At an extreme, this denial, splitting, and projection lead to a homogenized experience of self and the leadership group and possibly to the unlearning context of "group think." Everyone comes to share one mind, as thoughts that do not match are disallowed and disposed of.

Jack, the founder and CEO of a major vending machine company, has been, for a number of months, faced with the presence of a new and aggressive competitor that is financed by a major corporation. The new competitor has been highly effective and Jack's company has lost 20 percent of market share. As a result, Jack has been hard to live with lately. He thinks that just about everyone is out to get him and that no one is doing their job right; after all, "They were all caught with their feet up." His first reaction was to fire one of his key people (a scapegoat) to send a signal to everyone else. His next step established unrealistic performance goals that were predictably not met which he then asserted proved that he was right—that no one wanted to or could get the job done. He then developed a reporting system that permitted him to micromanage virtually all aspects of his company. Every layer of management between him and the route drivers no longer felt needed. Jack made it clear that hereafter he would do all the thinking and call all the shots.

Jack unwittingly adopted the mastery response to control his anxiety, and in the process projected his paranoid and distorted thoughts onto his employees, who now have to be watched every minute (like little children).

Projected Feelings   Leaders of large organizations must feel that they can lead their organization to great success. They must believe that they can overcome great odds and win in the end. They must believe that they are competent, capable, in charge, and worthy of being respected and admired. They must believe that they are relatively invulnerable to failure as well as rejection. They must believe that they can overcome individual, group, and organizational resistance and lead everyone to fulfill their great vision for the organization. It is, therefore, important for them to dispose of feelings that do not support this grandiosity. Feeling vulnerable, limited, unworthy of admiration, imperfect, and unable to lead or fight back against problems, competitors, and resistance must be disposed of. Feelings that cannot be repressed or suppressed are unconsciously projected onto others who then feel vulnerable, limited, imperfect, and in desperate need of saving by a caretaking leader.

Once again, it is readily observed in large organizations that members of management and, in particular, the CEO assume a paternalistic (or maternalistic) role under which everyone will be taken care of but only if they become unquestioning, admiring followers. In particular, leaders often appear to feel that only they should be in control and only they can get the job done right, something many followers may also unconsciously desire.

William has been appointed to a role where he is responsible for managing a new department that has performance problems. He is unsure of himself and incredibly anxious about his ability to turn the department around within the time limits imposed by his boss. As a result, he has become extremely irritable and recently kicked a trash can across a large room in full view of many of his employees. He has been heard to slam doors and yell at several of his subordinates. The easily demonstrated lack of progress in his department, combined with a recent negative evaluation by his boss, has him running scared and he has become exceptionally angry and irritable—feelings and actions that he disclaims despite obvious evidence to the contrary. In fact, he asserts that those who report to him are the ones who are really angry about how their department and they have been treated and that they are bound and determined to make everyone's life miserable, including William's. Their resistance to change in the form of passive aggression, William asserts, has undermined every one of his initiatives to improve the department's performance. In this case example, William has disowned his feelings and accompanying behavior by denying that he is angry and irritable and projecteing them onto everyone else who he then asserts are the ones who are angry. This has created a departmental culture in which feelings of anger and fear of failure cannot be discussed.

Projected Attributes   Personal attributes are also selected to reinforce the perception of the leader as nearly perfect and in absolute control, and attributes that do not fit this self-image are disposed of. Attributes which leaders disclaim are the lack of sufficient skills, knowledge, and experience to lead; insensitivity to others; unpredictability; lack of planning; and unilateral authoritarian tendencies to be dominating and controlling. Other traits that are frequently disowned are arrogance, vindictiveness, perfection, and vanity. All of these personal attributes are often projected onto others, who are then thought to be inexperienced, ignorant, controlling, arrogant, vindictive, critical perfectionists and always want something to fulfill their vanity or self-interest. The leader who knows others to be like this will, ironically, create a self-fulfilling prophecy in which he or she becomes more anxious, paranoid, arrogant, or vindictive in response to pathologically certain knowledge that others are incompetent or out to get or take advantage of him or her.

Jill is in charge of a department that makes a critical subassembly for a major product of her company. She is intent on proving to everyone that she deserves her job and, in fact, a promotion. She has become preoccupied with making sure every subassembly is perfect, which has translated into a need on her part to control just about everything in the workplace. Everyone is painstakingly trained, supervised, monitored, evaluated, accounted for, and, in general, micromanaged. Every subassembly is inspected twice, and she further inspects a fair number of them plucked off the assembly line at random intervals. She has just about driven every employee over the edge with her constant nitpicking criticism, even though performance reports for her department's work are the best in the company. To Jill, their work is never quite good enough or fast enough. However, when she is confronted over her micromanaging behavior she claims that she is not a perfectionist or "control freak" and is just trying to do a good job. If pressed, she often retorts that her superiors are the ones who are the perfectionists and set deadlines and specifications for her department that are unrealistic and that her employees fail to meet. Her actions have created a departmental culture in which Jill's distressing and often punitive and denigrating criticism is not open to inspection. As a result, employees feel that there is little hope of change, and they are unhappy.

The Shaping of Followers through Projective Identification

Projective identification involves the unconscious taking in (introjection or incorporation) of the projected thoughts, feelings, and attributes of others. Mary, who is angry, may suddenly assert that it is actually a friend or colleague (James) who is angry ("I am angry because you are angry with me and you have made me angry by your angry behavior"). This often sudden assertion is frequently accompanied by complete certainty. As a result, Mary rapidly feels much less angry and acts less angry, while at the same time demanding an explanation of why James is so angry with her. At this point Mary's anger has been denied, split off from herself, and projected onto James. If James begins to feel angry and then act angrily (in part as a response to being treated as though he is angry), the projected anger is understood to have been introjected by James (projective identification). He now possess Mary's anger, which then validates Mary's assertion that he is angry.

Given this unconscious interpersonal psychodynamic, it is easy to see how a powerful authority figure such as a CEO or senior executive can promote introjection of his or her projections by employees. In the examples that have been given, employees may be continually treated as though they are untrustworthy, ignorant, inexperienced, incompetent, angry, depressed children, and generally unable to be effective. The CEO and leadership group can reinforce these projections with such actions as micromanagement, top-down decision making, and unilaterally imposed downsizing, restructuring, and reengineering. These actions affect all employees, but leave them out of the process, thereby promoting a sense of devaluation, vulnerability, and dependence. It is therefore easy for employees as a group to introject the CEO's and senior management's projections onto them; that is exactly how they are being treated, and if they are being treated that way, they must be that way.

In sum, top management, via projection and accompanying actions, can powerfully influence employees in the direction of integrating their projections of inadequacy, ineffectiveness, and vulnerability. Projective identification, therefore, becomes a central ingredient in developing what is often the traditional quality of leader/follower relations in the workplace.

The Shaping of Followers through Executive Transference

Transference is an important and complex unconscious psychodynamic. It is also a process that interacts with projection. Transference involves the unconscious transfer of prior life experience and accompanying feelings or fantasized internal object relations onto a contemporary situation or interpersonal relationship (Diamond 1993; Ogden 1990; Tansey and Burke 1989). The result is that the individual comes to know here-and-now events and relationships in the same way prior relationships (real or fantasized) were known, experienced, and felt about, which encourages the same responses. An abused child who feared a parent may readily experience workplace relationships as containing many elements of the relationship with the abusive parent (demanding, controlling, judgmental, punishing, withholding) and respond with feelings of fear and withdrawal or dependency in dealing with a superior in the workplace. Similarly, anxiety-ridden childhood interpersonal relationships may have promoted a mastery response, in which the child tries to please parents in order to control them and receive approval and love by more perfectly meeting their expectations, or perhaps abandoning the receipt of approval and love and fighting back against them. Were this individual to become a CEO or executive, rejecting, resistant, and demanding behavior on the part of subordinates that promotes uncertainty and anxiety might be met with overwhelming feelings of needing to get control. Transference, in this case, unconsciously creates the context for knowing, experiencing, and feeling about the present (in terms of the past or in fantasy), which then provokes excessive or disproportionate anxiety and psychologically defensive workplace practices such as mastery.

Employees may come to know that the executive responds in an unpredictable and disproportionate way to their actions and workplace events for no apparent reason other than "That's just the way he or she is." A "hot button" has been pushed, which has resulted in workplace actions that are inconsistent in many ways with an intentional response to the event or interpersonal relationship.

In Sum: The Shaping of Organizational Dynamics by Executives

CEOs and executives are the dominant individuals in the workplace and, as a result, they have a powerful influence upon the workplace, employees, and work, some of which is driven by unconscious needs to master their own anxieties. As a result, they unwittingly defend themselves with splitting and projection and are vulnerable to transferring prior life experience and feelings onto the present, especially when the present is filled with problems, threat, and anxiety. It is also natural for employees to introject executive projections, thereby completing the self-fulfilling prophecy and creating an unconscious balance in the workplace that constitutes the organization's intersubjectively created identity and culture.

THE INTERACTION OF FOLLOWERS WITH LEADERS

An assumption usually made about leaders is that they have strong personalities that permit them to be visionary, self-directed, mastery oriented and able to shape organizations and lead people (Bennis 1989; Srivastva 1983). However, executive leadership style and behavior can also be understood to be a product of unconscious interpersonal and group dynamics focused upon executives in the workplace that go unnoticed and unreported by executives in a clinical setting (Baum 1987; Diamond 1993; Schwartz 1990; Turquet 1975). Executives hold focal roles of power and authority which, when combined with the personality tendencies that permitted them to acquire the roles, often attract unconscious attention (Czander 1993; Hirschhorn 1988; Tansey and Burke 1989). These dynamics require revisiting workplace projection, projective identification, and transference to more fully understand their powerful influence upon executives.

The Shaping of Executives through Employee Projection

Employees are invariably provoked to many different feelings toward leaders, many ways of thinking about, knowing, and understanding leaders and many ways of "dealing" with leaders. Leaders are often remote and hard to get to know as people and, as a result, employees are prone to "make them up" in their minds and then treat them as though they are that way rather than understanding leaders for who they are. This process contains and even promotes splitting and projection of thoughts, feelings, and personal attributes on the part of employees.

Projected Thoughts   The notion that the thoughts of individuals can be attributed to or projected onto others has been discussed. Thoughts that are paranoid, erratic, inconsistent, poorly formulated, and inconsistent with performing good work are often disowned by those who have them. They are then recognized in others onto whom they have been projected.

Thomas does not think anyone else is competent. He believes that management is incompetent and untrustworthy, and that they frequently sabotage his work by providing him with misdirection. These arrogant and paranoid thoughts make him feel anxious and that it is necessary to protect himself by trying to make sure that no one is in a position to evaluate his work. As a result, he is hard to supervise and makes it difficult to assess his work by constantly changing his work methods. However, despite his untrusting, arrogant, and contemptuous thoughts, he tells others that he is an open, trusting, nonjudgmental, and friendly person. Everyone who works with him has come to accept the paradox between how he acts and what he thinks. Thomas is able to maintain this paradoxical thinking by splitting off and projecting his arrogant and paranoid thoughts onto others, including his boss. This leaves him feeling that he is not untrusting, arrogant, or paranoid. At the same time he is absolutely certain (pathologically certain) that those in charge have to be watched every minute because they do not know what they are doing and they are devious and arrogant enough to try to tell him what to do.

Projected Feelings   Feelings can be projected onto others. Someone who is frightened or angry may not own these feelings preferring rather to place them into others. Joan, who is an accountant, heard that an unanticipated analysis of a potential merger was expected by the Board at their quarterly meeting, which was only a week away. Joan immediately spoke to Harry, the Assistant Vice President of Finance and her boss, to confirm the rumor. She knew it would usually take weeks if not months to prepare. During the meeting, Harry revealed that he had known for some time that the analysis might be needed but that he got started too late preparing for the meeting. Joan masked her anger and frustration about the crisis by a calm expression of her irritation to Harry. She and her staff, she said, would have to work nights and the weekend to develop the analysis. Harry's response was to assume an attitude of aloofness and indifference, and he did not apologize to Joan. Joan, upon returning to her office, felt enraged, threw her portfolio on her desk, and left for lunch early.

Before continuing, it is important to note that Joan's anger, as will be discussed, is influenced by the transference of angry feelings from the past onto the present. Joan was frequently abused and humiliated by her parents, which makes her excessively sensitive to this type of behavior on the part of Harry. She also learned that feeling angry is bad. As a result, she feels furious about Harry's treatment of her and unconsciously conflicted about openly expressing her feelings of anger. Denying and disposing of the anger becomes essential, and projection is a viable disposal mechanism.

During lunch, Joan reflects on her interaction with Harry and begins to realize that Harry is an angry incompetent fool who is trying to "piss her off and get her to resign." Her ruminations turn to thoughts that the next time she sees Harry she will really let him know how poor a manager he is. When she returns to work, her feelings of anger are diminished, having been vented in fantasy. Her anger was projected onto Harry in fantasy, who was then punished and humiliated, thereby making her feel better. If Joan is unsuccessful in coping with her anger and her relationship with Harry continues to be filled with tension, her internal fantasy world will begin to influence her behavior. Joan may begin to act as though Harry is always angry, as well as arrogant and contemptuous (partly a product of her projections). Harry may also come to feel angry (projective identification) which validates Joan's projection and encourages future projections. This permits Joan to feel hurt and victimized by "bad" Harry's intentionally painful acts.

Projected Attributes   Personal attributes may also be located in others. An employee who is a perfectionist and invariably critical of others may have learned as a child that he or she is not a person who is worthy of being loved (no matter how perfect he or she is). As a result, the employee does not know him- or herself to be worthy of love. Loveworthy aspects of self are then splitoff, denied, and projected onto others to maintain this self image. It should also be appreciated that those onto whom these attributes are projected may have a projective "hook" to pick them up. Many people are, from time to time, sensitive, caring, and loving.

Sally, one of Hogann's best employees, invariably thinks of herself as not being a nice person. She sees herself as an autocratic, impersonal perfectionist who becomes vindictive when crossed. She feels everyone else is nice except her. She is, however, an effective worker and gets her assignments done on time, but accomplishing this makes her constantly irritable and occasionally aggressive and threatening when her work is falling behind. She thinks of herself as bossy, abrasive, and unlikable ("Who could like someone like me?"). In contrast, she invariably finds her superiors and others to be friendly, supportive, and lacking her antisocial qualities. This bipolar black and white conception of self and others is a good indication that splitting and projection are at work. In Sally's case, in order for her to be effective she feels that she has nothing to lose by being assertive and at times aggressive (after all, she has nothing to lose because she is not worthy of being liked or loved). She does not see herself as friendly and supportive in her role and, as a result, splits off the friendly social aspects of herself and projects them onto others who are known to be friendly, not aggressive, and worthy of being liked and admired.

The Shaping of Executives
through Projective Identification

Executives are constantly confronted with subordinates who unconsciously wish to alter them via projection. They are encouraged by employees to become like the projected idealized or despised images that the employees hold for them. At the same time, executives do possess the desired images to some extent (the projective hooks). Thoughts, feelings, and attributes of executives that are inconsistent with the idealized or despised image held by employees are ignored, denied, or rationalized away. A serious avoidable mistake may be understood by employees to show that the executive is human and vulnerable rather than unprepared or incompetent. At the same time, executives unconsciously try to accentuate those aspects of themselves which are held in high regard by subordinates and suppress less than ideal aspects of themselves. The executives, in their unconscious pursuit of fulfilling the idealized or despised image of them held by workers, are rewarded by them for changing their personality and leadership style. As a result, some of the executive's personal attributes are unwittingly minimized and others accentuated.

It is, therefore, understandable that an executive may come to know him- or herself to be a remote, hostile, and unlikable authority figure who is excessively critical and controlling if subordinates constantly think, feel, and act as though he or she is. It must also be acknowledged that the executive will have some of these tendencies and may come to be known to be motivated in ways similar to, for example, self-centered, punitive, and controlling parental figures or other executives. In sum, if employees think that the executive is good or bad, and this differs from his or her self-awareness and self-image, it is easy for the executive to feel that he or she is out of touch with his or her personal motivations that produce the type of behavior asserted to be the case by employees. After all, can this many people be wrong?

A related aspect of projective identification is that once projections are taken in by the executive, an ongoing collusion to sustain the dynamic may exist. The subordinates wish to maintain their projections to feel good about themselves and in control of the executive in their minds. The executive, who is adrift in a sea of projections, introjects the projections and unwittingly comes to experience him- or herself in a manner that is consistent with the projections. The gradual addition and loss of parts of him- or herself (to become like the idealized or despised projected image) eventually creates a new workplace person who may not want to change. An executive who believes that he or she is a punitive perfectionist and not a "people person" may eventually lose touch with friendly and nonjudgmental aspects of self, further decreasing the likelihood of change. In sum, projective identification has an ongoing and powerful influence upon how executives know themselves to be as persons and leaders.

The Shaping of Executives through Employee Transference

A male executive may begin a conversation with a female employee in a tone that she perceives to be like her father's when he was being angry and judgmental with her. His tone and manner are immediately and out of awareness associated with how she was treated by her father. She also learned that she had to silently suffer through her father's behavior out of fear of punishment. As a result, this woman feels helpless as an adult to deal with her feelings, and becomes anxious, defensive, and frustrated. Consequently, her reaction to her boss may have little to do with what is going on with him at the moment. She immediately and out of awareness resorts to how she reacted to her father and becomes silently enraged and passively aggressive. The executive is unconsciously transformed into the punitive father and treated accordingly.

In Sum: The Shaping of Executives and Organizational Dynamics by Employees

Understanding projection, introjection, and transference creates new insights into understanding interpersonal workplace dynamics. Executives and, in fact, anyone in the workplace may be attributed feelings and attributes that, while somewhat like the person, are steadfastly maintained to be the person. Projection, introjection, and transference introduce irrationalities into the workplace that are hard to understand and detect and can be expected to create confusion and difficult interpersonal dynamics. Executives may come to be known by many based only upon the sum of all employee projections (an intersubjective identity). Executives may then be understood to be included to become personally disorganized via the unconscious process of projective identification.

SUMMARY

This chapter has examined organizational culture and its precursor, unconscious organizational identity. Organizational culture is unwittingly shaped by the many unconscious but profound aspects of the psychologically defensive workplace. These elements are understood to create organizational dynamics that contain, at their core, the psychologically defensive responses to anxiety: mastery, love, and freedom.

The chapter has also addressed another side of unconscious psychologically defensive organizational dynamics, that of the traditional psychological defense mechanisms of denial, splitting and projection, projective identification, and the unconscious context-setting nature of transference. Executives, it has been noted, unconsciously shape their subordinates into what they need them to be in order to perform their anxiety-filled roles. They also develop part of their personality and management style from their employees who, out of awareness, manipulate their perceptions of these executives in their minds to fit their childhood experiences of authority figures. It is therefore critical to appreciate that employees may not be responding to an executive for who he or she is and how he or she acts, but rather more as an object onto which current experience is projected or prior life experience is transferred.

It must also be appreciated that, in the rich milieu of out-of-awareness projection, projective identification, and transference, executives also try to pull desirable projections and transference from those with whom they work. An executive who symbolically holds his or her hands behind his or her back and asks an employee to guess which one holds the answer or reward (a pay increase, promotion, or additional organizational resources) encourages the employee to feel childlike, thereby putting the person in touch with childhood experiences in which the child was manipulated into guessing which hand a cookie was in. The projection drawn from the subordinate is associated with the powerful and controlling parental figure. Understanding how those around an executive are encouraged to feel about the executive is also an important way of understanding what the executive's unconsciously held ego ideal is.

To the extent leadership styles and executive personalities are, in part, shaped by processes such as these, leadership, it may be understood, contains an element of contingency or even chaos. People are selected for leadership roles based upon the leadership style that organization members feel they need. The result may be a search for an other who possesses suitable projective hooks onto whom or into whom may be unloaded all manner of unconsciously held negative or positive feelings and fantasies about power and authority. The leader might be selected for autocratic attributes and then pressed into autocratic behavior by passive and dependent subordinate behavior. The leader might be selected for caretaking, soothing, even loving qualities that it is felt are needed to control the destructive behavior of employees who may also feel that they need to be healed after being brutalized by a tyrannical former executive.

Last, it must also be appreciated that executives also rely upon projection, projective identification, and transference (Kets de Vries 1979). They come to know their subordinates in ways that they are not, but act as though they are. This process may result in the assumption that subordinates are just like little children who need to be watched, and the employees, having been infantalized and discounted, often begin to act immaturely thereby incorporating the executive's unconscious images of them.

THE LARGER CONTEXT

7

The Workplace and Society

> For the individual in an organizational role, extrapolation from his small, limited, and fairly insignificant world to the vast issues before us and our societies is not merely legitimate or simply desirable. It is essential in our search for the missing connections behind the experience of being lost in familiar places.
>
> Shapiro and Carr 1991, 180

> The work of dreams (and of dreaming) and of culture derive from the same unconscious source. At times, the unconscious might be better observed, less obstructed by defense and secondary process, through the analysis of dreams than of cultural materials. Yet this does not always hold. Dreams and dream interpretation are themselves shaped by and borrow from cultural materials—they are part of dreams' disguise and later secondary revision; in this sense, dreams are culturally constructed or constituted.
>
> Stein 1994, 5

All organizations exist in an open system with their local community, nation, and the world. They are influenced by the social culture in which they exist and simultaneously contribute to its creation. This is particularly true of local cultures and, in the case of large corporations such as Chrysler (which had to be bailed out by the government in order for it to survive to fulfill a greater good), their influence can extend to the nation. Large corporations also have an effect upon the world community, in which they may, for example, become a dominant influence in a small, under-developed nation; arrogantly dump hazardous products abroad which kill, maim, and make ill the citizens of other countries; or, in the case of huge multinational corporations, become a dominant global influence.

Our organizations are also influenced by the culture in which they exist. The management methods and values that are relied upon by executives are often unique to a region of a country or a region of the world. American management methods are often compared with those employed in non-western countries such as Japan. And, certainly, there is world-wide competition that inextricably ties together every organization with every other organization on earth.

Our organizations also take within them (across their organizational boundaries) the lives of their members, which are in large part lived outside of the organization, thereby introducing a side to organizational life which is constituted from life experience outside of the workplace. At the same time, it is at this joining of people with the workplace that workplace influences also pass beyond the boundaries of the workplace and into the family and surrounding community, with positive and negative effects.

In sum, organizations and local, regional, national, and even global society are interactive. Each influences the other in many small ways and occasionally in major ways. It is therefore important to explore the unconscious nature of the workplace and the unconscious aspects of society as part of an interactive whole. In this regard, attention must be given to the relationship between the workplace and the family and, secondarily, the local community, for it is within these variables much of the interaction exists. However, also to be discussed in this chapter is the relationship of the psychologically defensive workplace with larger society and the world and its history.

The following discussion is informed by the model of the psychologically defensive workplace. Just as some organizations and their cultures are dominated by one of the defensive practices of mastery, love, or freedom, so it may be true of regions of a country and of nations (lest we forget the master race of Nazi Germany). Our discussion begins with the workplace and its relationship to the family, two which coexist interdependently. Next, the workplace and the surrounding community are discussed for their interrelationships. The relationship between the workplace and the country in which it resides is examined and, last, the relationship between the workplace and the world is explored. The focus is on the contribution that the model of the psychologically defensive workplace makes to understanding the vast, complex, and ultimately indescribable nature of these relationships. The sweeping nature of the issues discussed do not permit much elaboration, as such constitutes the basis for another book. However, indications of the linkages between the psychologically defensive model of the workplace and the world beyond the workplace are provided.

THE WORKPLACE AND THE FAMILY

Much has already been said about the origins of the psychologically defensive tendencies and childhood development. Karen Horney notes,

But through a variety of adverse influences, a child may not be permitted to grow according to his individual needs and possibilities. But, when summarized, they all boil down to the fact that the people in the environment are too wrapped up in their own neuroses to be able to love the child, or even to conceive of him as the particular individual he is; their attitudes toward him are determined by their own neurotic needs and responses. In simple words, they may be dominating, overprotective, intimidating, irritable, overexacting, overindulgent, erratic, partial to other siblings, hypocritical, indifferent, etc. It is never a matter of just a single factor, but always the whole constellation that exerts the untoward influence on a child's growth. (1950, 18)

These kinds of family dynamics result in the lack of development of self-worth, security, and belonging and, in their place, the development of profound insecurity and a pervasive, vague apprehension relative to oneself and others; what Karen Horney refers to as *basic anxiety*. The child feels isolated, helpless, and alone in a world that is experienced as unpredictable, unnurturing, and potentially hostile. Basic anxiety blocks the child from successfully relating to him- or herself and others in a spontaneous expression of his or her true feelings (attachment and abandonment anxiety abound). Rather, the child is obliged to unconsciously cope with his or her feelings in a way that does not provoke more anxiety, and hopefully allays it. This leads to the three compulsive compromise and reaction formations: rebelling and fighting back (mastery in the form of perfectionism, arrogance, vindictiveness, and narcissism), clinging (love and dependency), or shutting others out (freedom and resignation).

The family setting may, therefore, be understood to potentially fill the workplace with individuals who are more or less prepared to successfully cope with the stresses and anxieties of daily work without becoming psychologically defensive and resorting to the psychologically defensive practices. However, it is equally important to appreciate that the workplace is filled with many of the stressors which reenact experiences of childhood and growing up. The workplace often contains dominating, overprotective, intimidating, irritable, overexacting, overindulgent, erratic, and hypocritical behavior on the part of leaders, executives, employees, and even consultants. If one assumes that any given employee received good enough parenting and subsequent life experience that promoted self-integration and self-esteem, the individual may, nonetheless, be confronted with extraordinarily stressful workplace conditions that provoke hard-to-manage aversive emotions (anger, fear, envy, contempt for self and others). These experiences encourage individual and interpersonal fragmentation that lower self-esteem and increase the likelihood of reliance upon psychological defenses and the psychologically defensive practices. In fact, individuals who have perhaps in some ways lived too sheltered a life (received good enough parenting) may be especially vulnerable to becoming personally disorganized when confronted with a hostile workplace.

In contrast, leaders, executives, and employees who grew up in dysfunctional families and who experienced equally unsupportive subsequent life experiences may find that a dysfunctional workplace is very familiar. They, in effect, come to work with many well-practiced psychological defenses and psychologically defensive practices ready for deployment.

Also to be appreciated is that, to the extent that the workplace contains serious dysfunctions that promote strong hard-to-manage emotions and psychological defensiveness, they are taken home across the workplace boundary to influence interpersonal relationships outside of work. Extraordinarily stressful situations lead to a gradual retreat from others as one's thoughts and feelings become focused upon and even consumed by workplace events, fears, anger, and anxieties. The old military expression, "If the military had wanted you to have a wife and children, they would have issued them to you," in some ways captures the essence of the workplace/family interface. Loss or diminishment of the "goodness" of supportive nonwork relationships may introduce additional anxiety into the individual, as well as strip him or her of a heretofore supportive resource that helped to allay it. In this way, the open systems and interactive nature of the workplace, the family, and one's life are locked together.

However, also to be noted is that if the workplace is supportive and nurturing and not experienced as threatening and filled with interpersonal or organizational insecurity, the individual who received good enough parenting will find it similar to prior life experience, but the individual who grew up in a dysfunctional family will not recognize it as familiar or even desirable and will unconsciously introduce his or her compulsive psychologically defensive tendencies into the workplace thereby creating dysfunction. These employees may be overly competitive and controlling, excessively passive and dependent, or highly invested in achieving personal autonomy. Relationships with others are experienced as containing threat when none or little exists; responding this way may provoke hostile and defensive responses on the part of others, which creates a self-fulfilling prophecy.

In sum, the family, one's personal life, and the workplace exist in a multifaceted embrace of immense complexity. In a sense, they are codeterminant, and thinking of them as discreet aspects of one's life experience introduces an artificial bifurcation that encourages simplistic compartmentalized thinking, feeling, research, and theory building. This fused perspective of life experience introduces the metaphor of the family as a way of understanding the workplace.

The Workplace as a Family

"We are all one big happy family" is a phrase that is often heard when discussing groups in the workplace, whether they be departments, divisions, or an entire organization. The workplace is certainly filled with family-like attributes. There are those who are in charge (the parents) and those who are dependent (the children). There are old, wise Board members, senior-level executives, and retirees to whom everyone looks for sage advice, not unlike grandparents. There are relatives in the form of other divisions, plants, and merged companies (in the case of a conglomerate or a horizontally and vertically integrated organization). There are, of course, many siblings who sometimes play and work together and sometimes fight and compete against each other for scarce resources and approval. Physical organizational spaces are also often laid out not unlike a home; there are cafeterias (kitchens), meeting rooms (family rooms), offices (bedrooms), official spaces such as board rooms (living rooms), work areas (basements and garages), and even parking lots (garages and driveways). Similarities also exist across a whole host of other family and organizational attributes, such as myths, stories, heroic deeds, idealized behaviors, thoughts and feelings, rules and regulations, planning processes, funding and budget processes, and so on. It is, therefore, very natural to experience the workplace as though it were a family. However, this is a metaphor that is also fraught with some difficulty, in that it seems to invariably imply a notion of family that is free of conflict and dysfunction (a happy family), which, of course, families and the workplace usually are not (Morgan 1986). In this context, then, the family metaphor puts forward an unrealistic notion of the workplace, or, perhaps more specifically, one that denies the existence of family dysfunctions in favor or creating or perpetuating an idealized image of a perfectly nurturing, conflict-free loving setting in which, coincidentally, everyone has roles to perform and does so perfectly and without direction, thereby eliminating the need for performance evaluation. In this regard, it is important to appreciate that the use of the family metaphor (and to this may be added the team or notion of a round table where everyone is equal) conceals the real nature of its functioning, in that it is a screen for paternalism and maternalism or, in other words, autocratic top-down control that cannot ultimately be questioned (like one's parents). It must also be appreciated that the image of an organization as a family also encourages unconscious transference of prior life experience onto the workplace, as well as the use of family-specific psychological defenses to cope with workplace anxieties. These outcomes must be viewed as distorting and as introducing influences into the workplace that are not adaptive to accomplishing work. A male executive who is treated just like his punitive father treated him will promote interpersonal anxiety rather than allay it.

The Implications of Family Counseling for the Workplace

To begin, it must be noted that family businesses constitute most of the businesses in the United States. They range from the very small business in which only immediate family members are involved to the very large, including publicly traded corporations dominated by family interests. In this regard, there is a tension between responding to organizational dynamics from the perspective that they must be understood to be business-like or that they are really family dynamics that are extended into the workplace. In practice, both considerations must be evaluated in the case of family owned and operated businesses. Thus, discussing the family as a metaphor for organizations is in some ways problematic, as it may, in fact, be the family (Morgan 1986). Therefore, understanding the implications of family therapy as they pertain to the workplace becomes all the more important.

The relationship between family-therapy precepts and those for organizational analysis overlap in large part in three areas. First, the nature of the roles assumed and assigned and how they are acted out are important in understanding organizational and family dynamics. Second, boundary making and management issues are implicit in organizations and families. Members must know who is in and who is out, as well as where the organization and family and its rules and influences begin and end. Last, family therapy often focuses on the unconscious development of coalitions of some family members relative to others (often triangles), which also occurs in the workplace.

Families are filled with roles that are usually not clearly defined and are often in constant flux due to the addition of new family members and their maturation. Nonetheless, roles have a powerful influence in family functioning regardless of their functionality. The workplace is also filled with roles, many of which are badly defined and articulated or not acknowledged to exist at all. When dysfunction occurs in either context, clarifying and articulating roles is helpful in making clear and conscious how family or organizational members are supposed to work and live together. Role clarification is, therefore, valuable to both families and organizations, although in organizations there is usually greater complexity and diversity.

Role clarification is enhanced by considering the psychologically defensive practices. Roles are not assumed, assigned, and acted out as part of an entirely logical scheme of family or workplace division of work. A role which contains power and the likelihood of being admired may be highly coveted by some family and organizational members who pursue mastery as a way of coping with their anxieties. Similarly, roles of dependency may be assumed, assigned, or imposed, and some family members may feel that they just want to be left alone and assume or prefer to be assigned few if any roles and to enact them in minimal ways.

Boundary management is an equally important aspect of family and organizational membership (Baum 1990). There are, however, some marked differences between families and organizations. Family members are members by default and cannot ultimately chose to join or leave, with the exception of joining by adoption, which may or may not lead to full incorporation into the family. In contrast, membership in organizations is voluntary for both the members and the organization as a whole, which may reject a member. This is an important difference when it comes to boundary management, although in a country like Japan organizational membership is often for a lifetime. However, the issue of developing and maintaining boundaries between the family and the organization and the rest of the world are similar. Clear boundaries promote certainty and allay anxiety. Organizational boundary management, however, must once again be acknowledged to be more complex because it involves managing boundaries between the organization and its task environment and also within the organization between divisions, departments, and functions—an issue that seldom has a counterpart in families.

Boundary management may also be understood to contain elements that can be illuminated by a psychoanalytically informed theory. Boundary management raises two issues. First, the setting of boundaries and their safeguarding contain important anxiety-allaying elements that are, in part, influenced by the three psychologically defensive practices. Second, boundaries introduce the notion of in and out (attachment and separation), and create the basis for unconscious group processes of projection, whereby group attributes are cast out and attributed to another group or nation. A family, group, organization, or country may be encouraged to collectively deny, split off, and project bad self-images onto an enemy. During times of war this form of good/bad split arises to support a society. The enemy is seen from a dehumanizing perspective that not only enables his or her destruction but makes is a moral imperative ("Kill a commie for Christ"). At the same time, those making the projection find themselves to be without evil intent and therefore good. This good/bad aspect of boundary management may also be described as a process of setting and safeguarding family and organizational boundaries, including psychological defensiveness.

The psychologically defensive tendencies of individual family and organization members or subgroups are often unwittingly enacted in the form of boundaries that are very real and must not be violated even though it is clear that other boundary conceptions are equally valid. Certainly, there are many boundaries that families, organizations, and societies share in common such as racial, religious, male or female, old and young, and, more recently, disabled. Issues of inclusion and exclusion preoccupy our society, organizations, neighborhoods, and families. These and many other attributes unique to families, organizations, and societies often contain elements of the three psychologically defensive practices. Issues of inclusion and exclusion can be manipulated to secure mastery over others or a role of dependence or autonomy.

A final consideration is the existence of coalitions of individual members that often spontaneously form to influence group dynamics and decision making. A parent may support one child while attacking another. Conversely, the children may seek the support of one parent over the other, or one child may seek the support of one parent to win out over a sibling who may seek the support of the other parent. Dynamics such as these have counterparts in organizations.

The vastly more complex workplace provides many additional problems, threats, and opportunities for coalitions to form, exercise influence, and disband. Psychologically defensive organizations are filled with many conditions that contribute to their psychologically defensive nature. When a coalition forms, all the previously discussed psychologically defensive group dynamics become operational. Coalitions may seek mastery (control), love (dependency), and freedom (autonomy).

All of these aspects of family and organizational dynamics are informed by the model of the psychologically defensive workplace, as family members and organizational members often cope with anxieties by relying upon the psychologically defensive practices. Family members and members of organizations often respond to anxiety-provoking interpersonal relationships and events with a compulsive pursuit of mastery (perfectionism, arrogant–vindictiveness, and narcissism), love (dependency and self-effacement), or freedom (being left alone and resigned behavior).

THE WORKPLACE AND COMMUNITY

When one journeys across the boundaries of the organization into the local community, a vast assortment of obvious and not so obvious powerful and benign influences are found. At one extreme is the very small family business that must adhere to many ordinances and pay taxes, but otherwise has limited interaction with the local community. At the other extreme is the large organization that may request and receive special advantages that contribute to its, and presumably, the community's financial viability. Businesses benefit their communities by providing employment and a larger tax base, contributing to civic organizations and by their executives and employees participating in local community groups and governance with an eye on improving their community. As a result, cities, counties, and states are locked in an intense rivalry to attract business and industry (of certain kinds) to their locale. Industrial parks have been created, and many tax advantages offered and conferred to attract business, employment, and, ultimately, growth. In sum, there are a number of important symbiotic interactions that occur around politics, regulation, the attractiveness of the community to employees, and social and religious values that must be considered.

Politics, Laws, Regulation, and Taxation

Local politics involves special interest groups in trying to influence the decisions of elected officials to benefit themselves. Politics is in large part a struggle for control (mastery), to receive something (love), or to be left alone (freedom). Laws and regulations and taxation are, of course, all open to the influences of politics, not only in their development but also in their interpretation and enforcement by government officials and employees. The model of the psychologically defensive workplace enables a better understanding of these forces of a political nature because similar forces exist in all organizations. Individuals, regardless of whether they are elected or appointed officials, public employees, members of special interest groups, or volunteers, all possess unconscious motivations and psychologically defensive tendencies that lead them to seek mastery, love, or freedom. Newspapers, journals, and television are full of reports of this or that person or group trying to get control of some aspects of government to get their way, receive something, or simply be left alone. Politicians are all too often narcissistic, arrogant, and willing to strike back when their pride is offended. In contrast, special interest groups strive to be taken care of and support anyone who promises to meet their needs. Possibly some of the most noteworthy stories fall in the area of being left alone ("Not in my backyard"). Individual citizens and citizen groups often challenge, by any means at their disposal, what their government does. In sum, the psychologically defensive practices can be observed to exist in the political arena and often lead to efforts to control local business. Also be considered is that businesses represent special interests that strive to influence decision making in the public arena.

Community Appeal

There are many objective, subjective, and, by extension, unconscious aspects to one's experience of one's community. Objective facts include appearance, property taxes, school districts, and the availability of community resources, such as public water, road maintenance, and shopping malls. On the more subjective and, therefore, unconscious side of experience, people may identify with a certain appearance of buildings, social culture, or history, and with people in their neighborhood. All aspects of one's world are perceived, experienced, and understood through the unconscious filter of subjectivity. The presence of a single run-down home in a neighborhood may provoke memories of an unsatisfactory, out-of-control childhood lived in poverty (a problem with mastery) and lead the individual to look elsewhere for housing. At the same time, individuals may seek a community where being left alone to do one's business is held as a high social value (freedom) or, conversely, where watching out for everyone else is the norm (love).

The nature of the local community will also affect the organizations within it. Many of the community's values are brought to work by employees or imposed by the community upon businesses. A community and its citizens who value autonomy can be expected to encourage their organizations to act autonomously.

Social and Religious Values

Social and religious values vary greatly between regions of large countries and within local communities. Some communities value a strong sense of mastery (large cities), while others may seek freedom from all outside influ-ences (cults and religious groups that reject norms, medicine, and technol-ogy). Not to be overlooked are desires to be taken care of by society or to take care of others as a social responsibility. There are also many types of religious beliefs and groups, some of which seek isolation or segregation from society while others seek to control it by imposing their unquestioned religious be-liefs and values upon their community and the nation via the political process. In sum, the influences of mastery, love, and freedom abound in the religious, social, and ethnic dimensions of communities and become part of the unques-tioned and unconscious culture that influences the thoughts and feelings of individuals, who then bring those thoughts and feelings to work.

THE WORKPLACE AND THE NATION

Every country has its own culture and accompanying norms, values, and ways of understanding and interpreting life experience. One's country heavily influences the workplace through its politics, laws, and regulations, its main-tenance of secure money and market systems, taxation, and such things as social services. This diversity must be acknowledged, but for the purpose of this discussion the focus is upon the United States.

Cultural influences have a clear impact upon the workplace. In the United States, unlike other countries, heavy reliance upon such perhaps faddish but rather brutal processes as downsizing, restructuring, and reengineering, is very likely a product of our unique culture, which focuses upon individual-ism, personal toughness, free enterprise, and capitalism (return on invest-ment). An announcement of a layoff of 50,000 employees by a huge corporation is often greeted by investors as a positive move, with correspond-ing increases in stock value.

Cultural values and processes such as these are foreign to many other na-tions and cultures, and herein lies the importance of appreciating the relation-ship of the workplace to the larger culture and nation. As in the case of community, several parameters merit examination: the public arena, national culture and history, and social and religious values.

Politics, Laws, Regulation, and Taxation

Many of the issues regarding politics, laws, regulation, and taxation are the same as for local communities. There is inevitably a struggle for control and mastery of the decision-making process that makes national politics what it is today: hotly contested and the subject of great skepticism. Special interest groups abound for the purpose of influencing legislation to their benefit, much of which is aimed at getting control of some aspect of their operating environment (labor law, product liability law), being taken care of in some way by the government (entitlement programs or trading barriers), or being left alone (freedom of expression and assembly or to possess and carry weapons).

These influences are ignored only at great peril, as indicated by the rising use of terror tactics by individuals and groups such as paramilitary organizations that resist public authority. Their values and beliefs are frequently attached to mutually shared unconscious and intersubjective group processes in which those who are members of a specific group come to collectively share the same thoughts and feelings, which readily leads to common action. The public arena also influences the workplace, and business organizations often develop associations that serve to lobby for favorable legislation.

National Culture

Nations have cultures that arise from their long histories. There are many cultural aspects to the United States. Themes such as independence, individual freedom, and a frontier mentality; capitalism and the need to get control of production to make a profit; taking care of the underdog (often a liberal concern); and cultural diversity are major elements of our culture. These elements and many more form the fabric upon which life in our country evolves and the web of shared relatedness that holds us together during good times and bad (Stein 1994). Our national culture clearly contains the issues of mastery, love, and freedom, which are at times unquestioningly pursued as an end in themselves. Our business organizations take in these many cultural influences (often slightly modified to meet the unique needs of the organization and its leaders), thereby becoming part of the larger culture. At the same time, our culture is influenced by big business trends (the stock market), management fads (downsizing), and financial management problems (bank failures, junk bonds, the savings and loan scandal), thereby creating a complex interactive whole that defies easy understanding.

Social and Religious Values

Countries develop their own social values and ways of customarily relating to each other, thinking, and feeling. Customary behavior in one culture may be interpreted as unacceptable by another. One culture may highly value personal autonomy and freedom while another may place high value on subordination of the individual for the greater good (socialist and communist countries) or contributing to the group (Japan). Within countries, there may also be different ethnic groups with their own subcultures and religions that may or may not be welcomed in the country and, if not welcomed, may become the subject of segregation or ethnic and tribal cleansing.

Many countries have a predominant religion (or perhaps none, as in the case of the former Soviet Union). Others have a diversity of religions which espouse many different values: not working on Sunday, supporting the local community, and, at an extreme, religious sects and cults that separate themselves from the national and local culture and religious beliefs. It is also clear that maintaining the separation of church and state is a tenuous proposition in the United States.

All of these diverse influences impact public and business organizations in a multitude of conscious and unconscious ways. Those responsible for operating these organizations are expected to meet the expectations of their society, including religious values, or otherwise risk being rejected. At the same time, business and public administration subtly influence national culture and religious beliefs, promoting immigration of groups with different cultures and religious beliefs.

THE WORKPLACE AND THE WORLD

Countries and their people are often very different from one another. They each have a national culture with its accompanying values and norms and ways of experiencing and interpreting life, work, and world events. This diversity is truly staggering when embraced. Today in the United States the diversity created by the melting pot and a nation of immigrants has become truly challenging. The notion of a butterfly flapping its wings in the Amazon affecting the climate in Siberia is becoming a known reality, one that always existed but was not acknowledged. The world and all of its nations, people, resources, and even its climate are a vast interdependent system. In this regard, it is important to locate the influence these interdependencies have upon the workplace, which affects the world community and, in turn, is affected by it.

Pervasive linkages of this magnitude and complexity are a sobering and perhaps anxiety-filled reality that stems in many ways from open-ended interpersonal relatedness. Just as people are linked together in this larger context, so are organizations. The success and fiscal well-being of organizations is linked to their nation's success, which is, in turn, dramatically affected by world-wide events, such as regional recessions, war, and natural disasters. The international marketplace is constantly growing and has already dramatically reshaped the world's economic community.

In sum, the people of the world and the many organizations that populate its surface are inextricably linked together in a hard-to-fathom embrace of unlimited interdependence. Understanding the dynamics of world-wide events may also be understood from the perspective of the theory of psychological defensiveness presented in this book.

Individuals, often leaders of nations, trading cartels, and massive international corporations can and often do have a profound influence on world events. A change of a few dollars in the price of a barrel of oil can destabalize economies with the possible threat of plunging much of the world into recession.

Events like hot and cold wars have major influences, both positive and negative. They may block trade and destroy economies but also create a market for those nations and organizations that produce expensive weapons systems. Those who lead these organizations and nations are each individually vulnerable to becoming anxious, psychologically defensive, and acting out the psychologically defensive practices. A despot may think nothing of invading another country or espousing a policy of ethnic purity. Their arrogance, vindictiveness, and narcissism are acted out upon the world stage. Similarly, one does not have to look much further than North Korea or Albania to find nations closed off from world events (the desire for autonomy and freedom). And there are of course nations that see themselves as relatively helpless in taking care of their own affairs, which encourages international meddling in the form of providing support, guaranteed loans, and favored trading status.

In much the same way that international events are shaped by the psychologically defensive practices, the interaction between these events and organizations are mutually determinant. Events in the world-wide community do have direct impacts upon the ability of organizations to acquire resources and convert them into a means of generating a profit. Large international corporations or cartels may also have a dramatic influence upon the world trading community. They may dominate segments of the economies of many countries, achieve the status of a monopoly provider of goods or services, and develop a major influence in the decision making of countries where they control a major part of the economy.

SUMMARY

This chapter has drawn attention to the open system in which our organizations exist. The system exists on a continuum from local to regional to national to, ultimately, the world and, perhaps in the distant future, the universe. Each of these levels of analysis offers insight into how organizations ultimately function and, in turn, the influence organizations have upon the public arena and local culture, including social and religious values. This chapter has stressed a complex and hard to document interactivity, while also emphasizing that the theoretical perspective of this book offers insight into understanding this complexity. The issues or themes of mastery, love, and freedom exist everywhere as a result of their being part of the human condition.

LEADING AND MANAGING CHANGE DURING STRESSFUL TIMES

8

If an executive demands that the people produce, he is exploitive. If he treats them with beneficence, he is paternalistic. If he is unconcerned about their worries, he is rejecting. If he opposes what he believes to be irrational, he is hostile. If he gives in, he is weak. Unlike his predecessors, he does not always know which way to turn.

Levinson 1972, 9

Managers, no less than other people, have personality quirks. Little things they do on occasion can drive their subordinates "up the wall." In the main, however, subordinates tolerate their manager's quirks because for the most part the manager's style is acceptable, and for many subordinates it is much more than that. But what happens to subordinates when a manager seems to be all quirks, when there is no in-between?

Kets de Vries 1984, 152

LEADING AND MANAGING CHANGE
DURING STRESSFUL TIMES

Organizations of the 1990s and beyond must operate in a constantly changing global marketplace filled with an ever-larger number of competitors. Change is the only thing that is assured. The ability to make adaptive organizational change is at a premium, and leaders and members of organizations are constantly being challenged to remain flexible. At the same time, they are faced with greater stress, which leads to hard-to-control anxieties about being successful. If the stress and anxiety are unrelenting, as is promised by the future, one might expect those executives who have the best psychologically defensive coping strategies to rise to the forefront as leaders (Diamond and Allcorn 1985). To the extent that this occurs, these leaders compulsively and unquestioningly pursue psychologically defensive leadership, organizational, and interpersonal strategies (Allcorn 1988). These strategies, while seeming to be adaptive, are not. They promote greater organizational dysfunction and anxiety, which encourages further and more compulsive resort to the psychologically defensive practices. This circularity of cause and effect are both the promise and threat of the psychologically defensive workplace for its leaders and their followers.

This chapter explores the implications of the psychologically defensive practices as they pertain to leaders and managing change. The adaptive and less-than-adaptive nature of the psychologically defensive practices is discussed. As a counterpoint to these dysfunctional aspects of leadership, a description of nondefensive, intentional leadership and followership is provided.

THE NATURE OF PSYCHOLOGICALLY DEFENSIVE LEADERSHIP

Entrepreneurs and leaders very often operate under extreme pressure to take risks and control people and processes to realize their grand vision for their organization. This sense of pressure comes from within the leader (he or she feels obliged to succeed) and from without (expectations of others, organizational problems, and opportunities that spontaneously arise). They, therefore, live their work lives in a context where great expectations are held for them by themselves and by others. As a result, they must be able to absorb, at times, open-ended anxiety surrounding risk taking innovation and the inevitable ambiguity surrounding decision making and managing others. This aspect of the lives of leaders at the close of the twentieth century must be fully appreciated in order to have empathy for the crippling effects of anxiety (and psychological defensiveness) that accompany carrying out their roles as leaders. Holding this in mind permits us to explore leadership and, in particular, various types or styles of leadership.

Leadership is the subject of an inexhaustible supply of points of view. Researchers, academics, and practitioners have developed many classification typologies of leadership. These schemes, however, fall short of explaining the psychological origins of leadership behavior. Understanding a leader's thoughts and feelings are critical to gaining a true appreciation of what motivates his or her behavior and leadership style.

CONTEMPORARY CLASSIFICATIONS OF LEADERSHIP STYLES

Many authors have provided informative leadership typologies (Astin and Scherrei 1980; Bassett 1966; Getzels and Guba 1957; Knezevich 1969; Lippitt

1969; Reddin 1970; Terry and Hermanson 1970). Some of the more familiar and interesting types of leadership styles are the following:

- Autocratic leaders make all of the decisions and pass them down to subordinates.
- Benevolent autocratic leaders make the decisions, but only after consultation with subordinates.
- Paternalistic leaders encourage employee dependence by withholding decision-making authority and resources and assuming a role as their protector.
- Authoritarian leaders make all of the decisions based upon formal organizational power and authority.
- Manipulative or pseudodemocratic leaders make all of the decisions, but then appoint committees to endorse them and give the appearance of participation.
- Bureaucratic leaders are low on task accomplishment and interpersonal style and prefer to use rules and procedures to enforce conformity.
- Hierarchical leaders communicate little, reward competitiveness, discourage openness and critical thinking, and frustrate needs for recognition and security.
- Entrepreneurial leaders are aggressive, risk taking, competitive, frank, and reward these attributes in others.
- Insecure leaders reward "apple polishing"; influence peddling and cronyism; discourage creativity and risk taking; and tend to create an atmosphere filled with gossip and manipulative behavior.
- Laissez-faire leaders leave decision making to their subordinates.
- Humanist leaders permit open communication, reward openness and critical thinking, discourage competitiveness and rivalry, and create a comfortable workplace setting.
- Democratic leaders permit employees to participate in decisions.
- Task-oriented leaders encourage initiative, cooperation, and competence, and usually create a work setting where employees feel secure and valued.
- Indigenous leaders involve others as needed and, from time to time, employees provide leadership.
- Integrative leaders are neither authoritarian nor laissez-faire, and encourage open participation under their direction.

This list does not exhaust all of the various leadership types that have been identified by researchers. It does, however, list many of the more familiar and common types that are found in the workplace. It must also be noted that these leadership styles, while providing insight into leadership, do not explain why leaders act the way they do. Leadership styles, while being contingent upon the circumstances of the moment, are also heavily influenced by issues related to interpersonal power and authority and personal needs to feel autonomous, liked, and admired. Leadership style is, therefore, based in part in the personality of an executive and its accompanying but not so readily acknowledged unconscious and irrational elements. Understanding the unconscious side of leadership returns us to the model of the psychologically defensive workplace.

THE PSYCHOLOGICALLY DEFENSIVE
ASPECTS OF LEADERSHIP

Thus far, leaders have been described as likely to adopt one or more of the psychologically defensive practices, some of the time or possibly much of the time. It has also been asserted that leaders both shape followers and are, in turn, shaped by them as part of an unconscious process of controlling others and events at work to control one's anxiety. Since leaders have such a profound effect upon others, organizational events, and success, it is important to revisit the psychologically defensive practices as they apply to understanding leaders or, more specifically, how, in many instances, they contribute to dysfunctional organizational dynamics.

The Appeal to Mastery by Leaders

The appeal to mastery, despite its adaptiveness to many situations, is nonetheless a compulsive psychologically defensive practice that has as its aim limiting the experience of distressing levels of anxiety. The leader believes that by pouring his or her highly mobilized and, therefore, nearly boundless energy into gaining control of the situation, anything can be accomplished and mastery can be restored. Feelings of weakness, helplessness, and dependency are detested. This appeal leads to three types of leadership styles. One of these styles will predominate; however, one or more of the others will occur with frequency.

The Perfectionistic Leader   The perfectionistic leader develops what he or she believes is a set of perfect performance standards for him- or herself and others that, if met, will lead to mastery of (control of) work and employees. This leader pays close attention to detail and is obsessed with order, rules, punctuality, and appearances. He or she also often possesses rigid and demanding moral and ethical standards that employees are expected to meet. Everything has to be just right according to the perfectionist's standards. In sum, this leader, by holding and trying to meet the standards (even if they have little to do with ultimately achieving success and may perhaps even inhibit achieving success), feels superior, which bolsters self-esteem, provides a sense of self-control, and creates a psychological and interpersonal platform from which to lead.

Large organizations have many members who strive for perfection in their work and who expect perfection from others. However, when it comes to the perfectionistic leader, not achieving perfection is not an option. Those that do not achieve perfection are usually singled out for special attention, remediation, and possibly termination. Therefore, the challenge posed by the unrelenting pursuit of control and perfection is to find ways to build upon their positive aspects while avoiding their compulsive, unquestioned use as a psychological defense. When a leader becomes overly perfectionist, controlling, and rigid, it is time to encourage the individual to step back from his or her work and examine his or her feelings. In particular, recent criticism (or threat of being criticized) and fear of failure may be the driving forces that mobilize perfectionism. It is felt that the painful criticism could have been avoided if things were just more perfect. When critical feedback is greeted defensively rather than as an opportunity for improvement, the perfectionist strives for mastery by regularly imposing perfection as a solution to the problem.

The Case of Perfect Performance

Ms. Jones owns a successful business that keeps her very busy. She also tries to supervise her favorite department for which she has little time. Her lack of availability, however, did not adversely affect the department until its manager unexpectedly quit and plunged the department into chaos: Work and employees began to be misscheduled, quality suffered and employee attendance became increasingly unpredictable as morale plummeted, and customer complaints surfaced and a number reported that they were ready to take their business elsewhere.

The department's growing problems were eventually discussed at a meeting of the executive group, and Ms. Jones was embarrassed. She promised that she would immediately take care of the problems. She met with her employees and emphasized that outstanding quality and work were expected. Having made her expectations known, she went on to say that she would be paying much closer attention to the department's operations.

She began to drop in unexpectedly to observe work. The smallest problem or minor deviation often led to a punitive discussion. As the weeks and months passed, Ms. Jones's campaign for excellence snared many employees; some multiple times. She began to develop detailed written procedure to guide every aspect of work. Despite some improvement in performance, department morale continued to fall. No one in the department appreciated having his or her work constantly scrutinized, and many began to be openly critical of Ms. Jones. Nonetheless, Ms. Jones steadfastly continued her campaign to get control of the work and employees.

Eventually, a number of supervisors and highly skilled employees began looking for new employment, which Ms. Jones was aware of but did nothing about. Her response was, "If it's too hot in the kitchen, then get out." Fortunately, a new manager was hired and no one left. Ms. Jones retreated back to her usual role of CEO and to the more distant oversight of the department.

Case Discussion

This is an all too common story of a hard-driving entrepreneur, owner, and manager who very likely achieved success because she was willing to do whatever it took to gain nearly perfect control of her company's production and distribution channels. In this regard, the compulsive pursuit of perfection is not all bad; however, it can begin to have a negative effect as companies grow. The owner cannot be everywhere all of the time. Trust and empowerment of managers and employees is essential. The perfectionist is highly intent upon cloning him- or herself so that everyone else is perfect, a strategy that is self-defeating and highly controlling. It also infantalizes employees and strips them of initiative, autonomy, and self-esteem. The result is a group of employees who only do what they are told and obsess over losing control of their work, imperfection, and criticism. These employees become risk aversive and take as much time as needed to gain as near as possible complete control over their work, time that is often not available in the marketplace.

The corrosive effects of a perfectionistic, critical, micromanaging executive are evident in the case. Employees, it is felt, must be highly controlled. Those who had autonomy under the previous manager chafed at the micromanagement and were ready to leave. Employees began to select in and out of Ms. Jones's department, which would have eventually created the workforce that has been described—risk aversive and obsessed with control.

It is also easy to see how Ms. Jones ended up shaping her employees in her mind. They were imperfect and their imperfection was creating operating problems (an irrational cause-and-effect relationship, although it appears to be the case). Imperfection is something Ms. Jones had, in large part, denied about herself, split off, and projected in this case onto her employees, thereby permitting her to easily recognize them as imperfect. Thereafter, they were treated accordingly. At the same time, the employees encouraged her unyielding and often times inappropriate pursuit of perfection by not openly challenging her. They may have, in part, denied, split off, and projected their competency onto Ms. Jones—after all, she was the owner and had to know. These dynamics are also enhanced by projective identification, in which Ms. Jones may have taken in the projections and felt not only perfect, but that it was her mission in life to achieve perfection. At the same time, the employees may have incorporated her projections of imperfection and felt to a great degree that they were unable to do anything right. It is, therefore, important to appreciate that unconscious processes have a role in creating these black-and-white workplace situations.

The Arrogant–Vindictive Leader   Arrogant–vindictive leaders seek vindictive triumph over others who offend their arrogant but delicate sense of pride. Personal weakness is not tolerated and competitiveness, winning, and getting even are highly valued. Anyone who crosses this leader understands that a competitive and combative response will follow, including the possibility of avenging rages and terminations. These leaders are dominating, exploitive, and willing to humiliate others because they are engrossed in an unconscious but unrelenting quest for power to bolster self-esteem and protect their false and arrogant sense of pride.

Organizations often have leaders who have a hard time controlling their anger when they are confronted with situations that are threatening to them and, in particular, employees who question their decisions and leadership style. This compulsive, mastery-oriented behavior, however, is beneficial given the right circumstances. It can be an important factor in the success of an entrepreneur who does not let anyone or anything stand in his or her way, including ethics. It is often tempting to place an employee with these attributes into situations where his or her arrogant pride and vindictiveness offers a ready solution to problems. For example, this leader's psychologically defensive practice may work to an organization's advantage when he or she is incorporated into a tough bargaining situation. His or her boundless energy and antagonism may wear down the opposition and, at the minimum, his or her eventual removal from the process will be experienced as a positive step thereby also possibly conferring a negotiating advantage. However, regardless of how tempting it is to use this person's psychologically defensive tendencies to the best advantage, it is better to help the person deal with his or her behavior.

The Case of Overpowering Leadership

Mr. Smith was hired as a vice president to develop a new product line. He had considerable experience developing similar product lines for other companies. He was very self-confident and it was clear from the start that he fully expected to achieve rapid success. He immediately set about his work with great energy, but it was not long before the going got tough. Every inhibitor he encountered he felt was a personal affront. His response was to invariably bear down harder on those in his way, which occasionally included threatening to get them fired. However, despite the turmoil, Mr. Smith succeeded in developing an outstanding product line. His many enemies, which he seemed to go out of his way to make, even acknowledged that he had accomplished what he had been asked to do.

Regrettably, Mr. Smith proved to be just as difficult to work with regarding day-to-day operations. He wanted to make all of the decisions and took on anyone who seemed to be usurping his authority. He remained highly combative and his behavior began to create serious workplace dysfunctions. No one wanted to deal with him, and every effort was made to conceal operating problems to avoid getting "nailed" by him. He was eventually asked to step down from his role as Assistant Vice President for the product line after a major sexual harassment incident with several female employees. This change was, however, publicly presented in a face-saving way as a new opportunity for him to develop yet another product line to which he was assigned.

Case Discussion

Case examples like this abound in organizations and often become part of their mythology. It is clear that power and hierarchy enable and perhaps in some sense unleash these psychologically defensive practices, in that, if you are the boss, who is to say what limits should be placed upon your behavior? If someone brings you bad news, why not fire him or her (kill the messenger)? Who is to stop you? Organizations are filled with these dynamics which, unlike with the perfectionist, are not so much aimed at controlling work as controlling one's sense of excessive false pride. Everyone must kowtow or face the possibility of being personally attacked and possibly fired. In a way, this is the stereotypical corporate bully who readily resorts to being threatening and intimidating.

The result is that no one feels that confronting the person is appropriate. It is, in fact, not safe to do so. The individual's ego must be fed good news, and problems must be either solved or suppressed before they get to him or her. This becomes the organizational goal, rather than taking risks to innovate and achieve excellence. Given time, this individual collects up around him or her one or more layers of sycophants who are willing to "suck up" to their boss but are often arrogant to their staff (often described as the "authoritarian personality").

These dynamics are also readily enhanced by the intersubjective shaping of employees and the boss. The boss despises personal weakness, vulnerability, and feelings of being worthless and not respected or perhaps feared. These feelings are denied, split off, and projected onto subordinates, who are then felt to possess these despised qualities and, therefore, may be aggressed and attacked because they are contemptuous and because, if they are this way, they are the perfect victim for the workplace bully. Employees may also encourage this behavior by denying, splitting off, and projecting onto their boss their sense of being proud of themselves and respected by others and their more aggressive qualities that permit them to fight back against their tyrannical boss. These dynamics are also enhanced by the incorporation of the projections (projective identification). The boss takes in the projections of being powerful and feared, which bolsters his or her self-experience of being all powerful and further supports his or her arrogant and vindictive behavior. The employees incorporate their boss's projections and feel worthless, helpless, and perhaps that they are responsible for being aggressed by their boss ("They deserve what they get").

The Narcissistic Leader   The narcissistic leader strives to be likable and appear visionary, competent, and a great leader, and therefore worthy of respect and admiration. He or she holds a magnificent vision for him- or herself and the organization and generates many ideas in support of this vision. However, once the organizational vision is explained, he or she prefers to let others worry about the messy details of implementing it. This leader, in order to secure narcissistic supplies, surrounds him- or herself with others who are dutiful appreciative, respectful, and loyal. This ensures the self-experience of being seen as great, highly admirable, and, if possible, worthy of devoted love. This is, in part, achieved by promising promotions, raises, and organizational resources. Those who do not respond are usually isolated, punished, and, if necessary, removed for not being "team players."

The Center-of-Attention Case

Mr. White was very pleased to be promoted to Director and placed in charge of a major program. His predecessor, Mr. Black, had built the program into one of the best in the company. Mr. Black had also been highly involved in community affairs and had received a lot of attention and accolades. Mr. White looked forward to having an active role in the community, which he felt would provide him the same positive attention as Mr. Black. However, within six months it was clear that the program's employees and many in the community were not welcoming him as he had hoped. This was, of course, irritating, and it threatened his vision of himself (ego ideal) as a great and admired leader.

He responded to what he felt was a cool reception by meeting one-on-one with many of his key employees to win them over. He made promises of promotions, raises, and company resources during these meetings to impress the employees and win their approval. In several instances, unresponsive employees were let go because they just did not seem to fit in anymore. Making good on these costly pledges eventually threatened the financial viability of the program. He also began to use program resources to entertain city council members, the mayor, and a number of influential business people in the community to win their approval and support. He was intent upon receiving the respect, attention, and admiration that he knew he deserved and that he was certain Mr. Black had received. Thankfully for the program, he was adept at gaining the sought-after respect and admiration and within a year the program was restored to its former profitability.

Case Discussion

Organizations often have leaders who have compelling needs to be admired and liked. These are all too human tendencies. However, when being liked and admired becomes a compulsive interpersonal agenda that leads to bending the rules and manipulating resources to gain respect and admiration, it is time to call a halt to the process.

The case describes a pattern of behavior that, once again, does not have the organization's best interests at heart. Mr. White seeks admiration and approval from others and will apparently do whatever it takes to achieve it. This results, once again, in a selecting in and out of employees. Those who are seen to be most worthy are the ones who fulfill Mr. White's vision of himself. Those who are less forthcoming are either discriminated against in terms of raises and other organizational rewards or, in the case of those who reject being manipulated in this way, terminated. This process gradually results in one or more layers of employees who are devoted to Mr. White and tacitly understand the rules of the road—keep him feeling good about himself by bathing him in adoring admiration and avoid bringing problems and messy details to him. It must also be noted that the employees who feed the process may themselves be in need of approval from others with whom they work. In some ways, they might be understood to be sucked dry of their narcissistic stores of good self-feelings in favor of focusing on making Mr. White feel good about himself (at the expense of their own feelings). They, in turn, end up looking to others and their family for narcissistic supplies to make them feel good about themselves.

A process such as this is also enhanced by denial, splitting, projection, and projective identification. Mr. White denies, splits off, and projects his less powerful and admirable qualities onto his staff, while they, in turn, are encouraged to deny, split off, and project their feelings of being empowered, powerful, and worthy of approval and admiration onto Mr. White. Projective identification, in a sense, seals the deal. Mr. White incorporates the projected images of himself as powerful and worthy of admiration, thereby further enhancing his sense of self. His employees incorporate the less-than-admirable qualities of Mr. White, which leaves them feeling relatively worthless and not deserving admiration. They must then look to Mr. White for leadership and direction as they no longer possess these qualities. At the same time, they must look to others to restore some sense of self as worthy and admirable.

Mastery in Sum

These three leadership styles are ways of seeking mastery over others and the situation to control the distressing experience of anxiety and low self-esteem. Failure to gain control threatens the leader with detested feelings of powerlessness and worthlessness, which are to be avoided at all costs. Flight from these feelings infuses the leader with boundless energy. Each of the case examples, while readily found in the workplace, provided a relatively pure type of example of the psychologically defensive practice. Certainly, there are many leaders in the workplace that are understood to be like the characters in the cases. However, work life is often more complex than these pure types. A perfectionist, if rebuffed, may, as a result of having his arrogant pride damaged by rejection of his or her standard methods, feel that it is absolutely necessary to get even (criticize) with the person who did the damage as a part of a process of self-vindication. A perfectionist may also, while tacitly understanding that he or she is not going to endear him- or herself to employees, seek the approval and admiration of superiors, colleagues, and a few subordinates to fulfill unconscious narcissistic needs.

The same may be said for the arrogant workplace bully who is willing to aggress anyone who injures his or her delicate pride or who gets in his or her way. The aggression may take the form of setting up perfectionistic standards that then permit unrelenting criticism and behind-the-scenes attacks. At the same time, the individual who has had his or her arrogant pride damaged may seek the admiration and support of a few people to make whole his or her narcissistic injury. Similarly, the narcissist may, upon failing to receive admiration and approval from others, turn on them without hesitation in an all-out battle of self-vindication to get rid of them. A part of this process may include the imposition of performance standards which resisters cannot meet, which lays them open to constant criticism, condemnation, scapegoating, and termination.

It is therefore important to appreciate these reinforcing linkages between the three leadership styles that comprise the appeal to mastery. It must also be understood that they may occur in rapid succession or simultaneously in many different ways, depending upon the situation.

The Appeal to Love by Leaders

Everyone silently hopes to be taken care of and have their self-esteem and security needs magically met. Leaders who appeal to love do not believe or, perhaps more importantly, feel that they are capable of mastery. They may, in fact, abhor overt dominating, manipulative, critical, and controlling behavior. As a result, they frequently let (encourage) others assume roles of leadership while hoping that they will then be taken care of by those who take charge in return for their caring and devoted support and loyalty.

The appeal to love results in the psychologically defensive self-effacing leadership style that is, in part, inconsistent with assuming a role of active leadership. However, a leader who puts the well-being of others first and creates a "warm fuzzy" workplace in which there is promise that everyone's needs will be met is frequently felt to be desirable. This is often the case after a mastery-oriented leader is replaced. Employees who feel that they have been aggressed, manipulated, and subjected to inappropriate uses of power usually react to an opportunity for a change in leadership by locating a new leader who will be gentle and caretaking (a people person).

This leader is not expected to and usually avoids taking charge and acting assertive or aggressive when it is appropriate. He or she also avoids dealing with disciplinary issues and conflict, preferring rather to ignore and suppress them. Issuing orders, assigning work, and appraising performance, actions that it is felt threaten to anger and alienate employees who are desired as friends and supporters, are avoided as much as possible. This leader stresses the organizational values of unselfishness, goodness, generosity, humility, acceptance of personal vulnerability, and sympathy, and hopes that others, when they take charge, will love and take care of him or her as per the espoused system of acceptable values.

What is important to appreciate is that the presence of a self-effacing leader often signals an entrenched group dynamic that makes change difficult. The leader is actively discouraged from changing, not only because of his or her unquestionable choice of a defensive leadership style but also because group members do not want him or her to change.

The Case of the Golden Lining   ABC, Inc. has been through some tough times. Its much loved and esteemed founder unexpectedly died without establishing a succession plan. The company's employees were distressed and unprepared for a change in leaders. An interim CEO, Ms. James, was quickly picked and she unexpectedly began to take charge, starting with a remodeling of the founder's office. Despite her interim status, she reorganized the management structure and established new company goals. Anyone who got in her way "got hammered into shape." No one was prepared for this, but no one openly contested it either.

Within months, many changes were made and Ms. James made it clear that she hoped to become the new CEO despite the fact she had been explicitly picked for an interim role. Eventually, several of the vice presidents and the Board confronted Ms. James over her behavior and she promptly resigned and decided to leave the company as well ("No one appreciated what she had to offer").

Careful thought was given to the selection of a new interim CEO. Mr. Younger was asked to take the role, and he accepted. He was charged with leading the company's employees through a period of mourning over the loss of their long-time boss who had hired many of them and seen many through hard personal times. In addition, everyone needed time to heal from the divisive battering Ms. James had delivered.

Mr. Younger set aside much of his time for one-on-one meetings with many of the key employees, and held open discussions with employees at lunchtime forums. He also developed social occasions which were well attended, modified a number of the objectionable changes made by Ms. James, and made it clear that he did not want to become the CEO, which cleared the way for a careful search process. However, he also avoided dealing with issues and operating problems, as well as problem employees. He just was not going to do it. Nonetheless, everyone was very appreciative of him and, in turn, they were more than willing to work harder and assume more responsibility (some of his responsibilities) in order to get the job done. There was a sense of organizational relief and healing taking place.

Case Discussion

Having one's dependency and nurturing needs met is certainly desirable and something everyone shares in common. However, when these needs become overdetermined and compulsive, they become the only important interpersonal agenda. This is certainly true in the case of *codependency* (Allcorn 1992). As illustrated by the case example, this is not an all-bad response to managing anxiety; however, it invariably forces others to accept leadership roles (once again, something that is not all bad and may become a developmental opportunity). This psychologically defensive leadership style works reasonably well, as long as the organization is not placed under too much stress. However, if organizational survival is threatened, there comes a time when the leader must lead or otherwise compromise survival. Others cannot, in fact, completely replace the designated leader during stressful times. There are, therefore, definite limits to how adaptable the appeal to love is for leaders.

It is also worth noting that, once again, denial, splitting, projection, and projective identification enhance these unconscious organizational dynamics. The leader denies personal qualities associated with mastery and wanting to be in control, being powerful and admired, and fulfilling a great vision. These are split off and projected onto others, often superiors and key staff who are then known to have these qualities and should, therefore, assume roles of leadership. At the same time, this leader encourages others to deny, split off, and project their more sensitive and caring qualities onto their leader while retaining their mastery-oriented attributes. Projective identification completes the process, with the leader accepting the projection of the caring qualities of others while employees accept the projection of the leader's mastery-oriented qualities.

The Appeal to Freedom by Leaders

Everyone may, at times, hope to be left alone. Avoiding others and problems is less stressful, but it comes at the cost of losing one's zest for living. Development is forfeited when personal goals and aspirations are minimized to avoid the pressures of accomplishing them. Leaders who are resigned make it clear that they prefer to be left alone and not pressured to solve problems or take the lead.

Ironically, this leadership style is encouraged by others who prefer an inactive leader who makes few demands, suppresses conflict, resolves problems by taking the line of least resistance, and ignores the real world in favor of developing a stress-free workplace. This leader also holds few performance expectations, which often contributes to low group morale.

The Case of Misdirection General Manufacturing, Inc., after a few years of operation, reached a point where a major reorganization was needed to address many unresolved growth issues. The company had flourished, which led to proliferation of specialized products and accompanying specialization among employees. It was agreed that the restructuring would be assisted by a consultant and would require the selection of a new CEO. The aging owner ruled himself out as a candidate for the role.

An extensive search ensued with the help of a search firm recommended by the consultant. The search firm interviewed all the senior executives in the company and learned that they wanted a dynamic, well-organized visionary leader to lead their continued growth. A number of good candidates were located and interviewed, but none were found to be acceptable. The search firm's representative was puzzled by this outcome. A second round of candidates yielded similar results. It was at this point that a colleague was put forward by several vice presidents. This individual was less qualified than the external candidates and, in fact, had a track record of accomplishing little in a role where much could have been done.

Mr. Dolittle's possible appointment as CEO was put up as a trial balloon and received a positive response from many of the executives and employees. The decision was made to offer him the position. He accepted and everyone was happy. The search firm's representative surmised that the company's leadership, while verbalizing a desire for strong leadership, enjoyed their autonomy and feared that the hiring of an experienced executive would undermine their power.

Case Discussion

The appeal of being left alone to do one's thing is powerfully seductive. Our culture strongly encourages individualism and a rugged, go-it-alone attitude toward accomplishing work. Contentious organizational dynamics often further support these feelings. At times, it may be dangerous to speak up and voice one's opinion. Interdepartmental rivalries and zero-sum incentive systems promote rampant interpersonal and interdepartmental competition, including many of the win–lose dynamics of the appeal to mastery. It is, therefore, not uncommon to find employees who prefer to be left alone to do their job exactly according to how the job description is written, which defends against unexpected and challenging task assignments.

The resigned leader is readily spotted and leads the group in flight from the contentious and stressful aspects of work and, in particular, innovation. This leader's ideological stand for being left alone resonates with many employees, who come to feel this way too when the organization is placed under stress, such as the need to downsize. As illustrated in the case, this leader is often preferred by senior-level executives and managers who receive little direction, although it may place the entire organization at risk.

These organizational dynamics are accompanied by denial, splitting, projection, and projective identification that reinforce the trend toward being left alone. The leader denies, splits off, and projects his or her controlling, demanding and coercive attributes and invasive caretaking qualities into others (often superiors) who are then readily recognized to be a negative influence and must be avoided. Staff may also be felt to possess these attributes, which leads to avoiding interacting with and directing them. The resigned leader, therefore, possesses a quality of paranoia about the intentions of others (not unlike the arrogant–vindictive leader, who thinks everyone is out to get him or her). Employees who work for this leader are encouraged to project similar feelings onto other executives and departments. The inevitable response, which in part fulfills the fantasy that others are out to control, dominate, direct, order about, set goals, and monitor performance, is that those who must work with this leader and his or her band of loners have to be insistent in order to be heard and frequently demanding in order to get desirable work accomplished. This becomes progressively more true (a self-fulfilling prophecy) the more resistant the leader and his or her employees become to accepting direction and being held accountable. They may also incorporate the projections made onto them, thereby experiencing themselves as being unfairly demanding, controlling, coercive, and otherwise a bad influence. As a result, these unconscious and overt organizational dynamics come to be acted out in a mutually reinforcing way.

MANAGERIAL CHARACTERISTICS VERSUS DEFENSIVE LEADERSHIP STYLES

Understanding the difference between the list of leadership types and the underlying motivations for their development is critical in appreciating the true complexity of dealing with leaders. Each of the defensive leadership styles can be matched to the leadership characteristics first mentioned.

The appeal to mastery and its three accompanying leadership styles (perfectionist, arrogant–vindictive, and narcissistic) may be grouped with the following leadership characteristics: autocratic, benevolent autocrat, manipulative or pseudodemocratic, authoritarian, paternalistic, hierarchal, and entrepreneurial. The appeal to love and its accompanying self-effacing leadership style may be matched to bureaucratic, personal, humanistic, and insecure. The appeal to freedom and its accompanying resigned leadership style may be compared to the laissez-faire leadership style. By comparison, the intentional leadership style discussed in the next section can be matched to the democratic, indigenous, integrative, and task-oriented leadership styles.

THE NONDEFENSIVE INTENTIONAL LEADER

Many organizations are blessed with good leaders who are highly effective. These leaders are not overly threatened by stressful situations and, therefore, do not become psychologically defensive or, at the worst, only minimally so. They continue to be able to think clearly and observe with reasonable objectivity what is going on around them. Additional characteristics of these intentional leaders are nondefensive acceptance of feedback, maintenance of self-reflective skills, sensitivity to what others are thinking and feeling, and a willingness to take risks and innovate in the presence of uncertainty. In particular, the mastery-oriented aspects of their personalities, while present, do not become compulsively relied upon to defend against anxiety; nor is dependence or freedom particularly sought. This leader advocates excellence without becoming preoccupied with achieving perfection. He or she is assertive without becoming aggressive, and employees are encouraged to learn to feel good about themselves as a result of accomplishing outstanding work. These leaders also discourage dependency and, while respecting individual freedom, autonomy, and interpersonal space, also firmly insist upon group participation and membership as well as meeting goals and being held personally accountable for one's work.

Organizations need this type of leader. The balance of the 1990s and the century beyond promise to be stressful times. Leaders who function with intentionality under stress will be at a premium. Organizations can help support the development of intentional leaders by acknowledging the need for them and by nurturing intentionality in their leaders, who all too often function in a setting where negative feedback is the norm.

PSYCHOLOGICALLY DEFENSIVE ORGANIZATIONAL CHANGE

Leading organizational change is invariably challenging. Change implies many things to organization members, such as loss of familiar work and workplace relationships, loss of one's career path (or worse, one's job), geographic movement, learning new work, and often having to perform more work of a greater variety and complexity as a result of planning and implementing change as well as a shrinking workforce. There are, therefore, good reasons why employees are not eager to embrace major change and often even minor change. The result is that when change is needed employees become anxious. Some may greet change as a challenge and see the glass as half full. They foresee opportunities for personal growth and advancement. Others, however, are often highly invested in their current jobs and hard-won interpersonal relationships. Change not only threatens these, it threatens them as people who feel competent, valued, and worthy of respect. These employees feel excessively anxious and become psychologically defensive. As a result, they become hypercritical of plans for change, antagonistic to those proposing or leading change, and develop greater needs for approval and admiration, which they fear will be lost if change occurs. They may become almost disconnected from events and highly dependent upon others to tell them what to think, feel, and do. They may also put up many barriers to block out acknowledging the need for change which is experienced as invasive and coercive. They just want to be left alone.

It is also worth noting that the maintenance of intentionality and the realization of the psychologically defensive practices anchor two ends of a range along which a bell-shaped curve exists. Most employees will be somewhere in-between, although they can be encouraged to be at either end of the range by top management's handling of change. Executives who permit sincere and meaningful employee participation in locating, planning, and implementing change encourage employees to become less anxious and therefore less defensive. However, there are many instances where executives approach change as an assault upon what they anticipate will be a resistant workforce. This predictably creates a self-fulfilling prophecy filled with substantial anxiety and resistance to change.

In sum, executives who are responsible for leading organizational change must attend to the levels of anxiety engendered by change. They can make decisions that encourage participation and identification with the organization and need for change. They can also cut employees off from participating and feeling valued, thereby promoting anxiety and alienation among employees from themselves and their aspirations, from each other, from management, and from the organization. Appreciating the nature of the psychologically defensive practices as they are played out relative to organizational change informs top management, thereby enabling leadership to implement change that minimizes anxiety and the emergence of the psychologically defensive workplace.

DEVELOPING NONDEFENSIVE LEADERSHIP OF ORGANIZATIONAL CHANGE

Changing psychologically defensive leadership styles is challenging and can be unrewarding. Complete success is seldom a likelihood. Direct confrontation threatens the leader, thereby making him or her anxious and reinforcing reliance upon the psychologically defensive leadership style. In addition, those closely associated with the leader will often defend the leader, which increases the risks involved in offering criticism or suggesting change. In particular, loyal followers will not want to give up their influence and the benefits they gain by being closely allied with the leader.

There are other avenues of pursuit. The leader may be approached one on one to discuss the effects his or her leadership style have upon the group and its members. The expression of these concerns, if heard, may open the door to self-reflection and change. External leadership training may be suggested as a means of improving the leader's performance. Intentional leadership may be modeled by others, which may influence the leader's subsequent behavior. Important decisions and the development of major systems, it may be suggested, might be deferred to a task group or committee for review and recommendation. This step avoids an immediate autocratic decision or no decision at all. A final consideration is the use of an organizational consultant who is trained to help leaders and groups deal with dysfunctional leadership styles and group dynamics. The consultant may, in addition to working with the leader, observe interpersonal and group dynamics that covertly encourage the leader's defensive style. This paradox is often present and blocks change on the part of the leader who may desire to change.

SUMMARY

Leadership is a complex subject that often overlooks some of the greatest and hardest to document and study complexities: the unconscious side of leadership that includes compulsively relied upon psychologically defensive practices. Any discussion of leaders and leadership is incomplete without taking into consideration the full spectrum of motivations that leaders possess when they are presented with a stressful leadership opportunity. This chapter has emphasized that while not all leaders are consistently vulnerable to experiencing excessive amounts of anxiety, many are, and they, to a greater or lesser extent, come to rely upon the psychologically defensive practices described here. Understanding this—the human side of leaders in the workplace—permits greater understanding and empathy when we encounter leaders who appear to be temporarily distressed, disorganized, or perhaps not their usual thoughtful selves.

CONSULTING TO CHANGE IN ORGANIZATIONS 9

Such a method [of understanding organizations], then, should require a student of organizations to fully describe an organization's concept, objectives, plans, its view of itself as well as its relationships with others, and its leadership. It must enable the consultant to understand systems of communications, coordination, guidance, control, and support. It must help him to delineate relevant environments and behavior settings. It must be a guide to unfolding the rationale of the organization, explaining its activities, and critically evaluating the organization's adaptive adequacy, followed by a reasoned series of recommendations.

Levinson 1972, 6

Many people learning consulting skills look for techniques, interventions, and procedural ways to be more effective as consultants. But there are special demands of the consulting role that transcend any specific methods we might employ, that contribute to our effectiveness no matter what our technical expertise. A unique and beguiling aspect of doing consulting is that your own self is involved in the process to a much greater extent than if you were applying your expertise in some other way. Your own reactions to a client, your own feelings during discussions, your own ability to solicit feedback from the client—all are important dimensions to consultation.

Block 1981, 11

Executives who coach and mentor employees and who serve as inside change agents, human resource professionals who serve as inside consultants, and external consultants need a frame of reference for understanding the psychologically defensive workplace. Unconscious avoidance of unavoidable workplace anxieties distorts thinking and feeling. Rational role enactment and intentional decision making are compromised, and this, in turn, becomes one of the focuses of a successful organizational diagnosis, intervention, and change effort. The psychoanalytically informed executive, human resource professional, or consultant must, therefore, be able to understand the psychological defensiveness that leaders, managers, and workers bring to role enactment and task performance in order to be able to change the psychologically defensive workplace.

This chapter explains how the model of the psychologically defensive workplace informs those who consult to organizations. However, maintaining this focus is not intended to mean that executives and other internal change agents cannot benefit from reading this chapter—they can. External consultants, executives, and human resource professionals are all faced with the same organizational dynamics and the need to change their psychologically defensive and dysfunctional aspects.

This chapter is divided into two parts. The first explains how to figure out what is wrong; to diagnose the organizational problems. The second part addresses how to successfully intervene to create organizational change. Each part relies upon the model of the psychologically defensive workplace and its contribution to understanding and changing dysfunctional organizational dynamics.

THE ORGANIZATIONAL DIAGNOSIS

Psychoanalytically informed consultation begins by negotiating an agreement for the consultation with top management, including their commitment to see it through and to pay the costs of the consulting engagement. The agreement is promptly followed by an orientation with management, communication of the consultation throughout the organization, and commencement of an in-depth confidential interviewing process of a broad cross section of the organization's employees. It is important to start immediately, as employee anticipation of the consultation process leads to uncertainty, anxiety, and the making up of information if it is not readily available.

When it comes to understanding the psychologically defensive workplace, taking one's time to develop a firm understanding by collecting information is in order (Levinson 1972). Many if not all of the members of top management, most of the middle managers and supervisors, and a cross section of employees should be interviewed. It must be explained that all interviews are confidential and that no one's name will be used in providing feedback or in preparing reports. This proviso is critical in order to achieve open communication with those interviewed. Many if not all sites should be visited in the case of a geographically dispersed organization. In large organizations, this may include hundreds of interviews and several consultants. Human resource professionals may be able to function in much the same way as external consultants. However, inside change agents will have difficulty assuring interviewees of the sanctity of the confidential interviews. Sufficient time and personnel must be committed to complete the interviewing process, preferably within one month in order to avoid the problem of sampling from a different organization as time passes.

A Note on the Interviewing Process and Its Implications for Intervention

Interviews of up to one hour should be conducted, using a preestablished list of open-ended questions that are germane to the organization and the context in which the consultation is taking place. Those interviewed should be allowed to talk at length if they choose to do so. Follow-up questions should be asked to clarify responses.

The interviewing process also begins the intervention process. The mere act of listening to what organization members have to say offers them an opportunity to verbalize (ventilate) their thoughts and feelings with someone who is interested in hearing what they have to say (Stein 1994). Therefore, interviewing is itself therapeutic, in that it validates employees as people worth listening to, something that may be lacking as a result of dysfunctional organizational dynamics. Care must also be taken to avoid excluding anyone who really wants to be interviewed, even if he or she was not originally selected for an interview. Doing the interview may yield important information and it demonstrates the patient and caretaking attitude the consultants bring to the work of organizational change. It should also be noted that some employees may say that they are representing the views of their colleagues or appear to be doing so, which should be validated by the interviewer. These interviews are often dominated by a "laundry list" of problems or grievances (sometimes written down). This must be taken in stride by the interviewer who must sustain a listening attitude by attending to the content of the list while also listening through the list for underlying content and meaning. During the interviews, special attention should be given to repetitive and psychologically defensively themes of a long-standing nature (Kets de Vries and Miller 1984).

The diagnostic work of learning from the interviews confronts the consultant with a fusion of the psychologically defensive practices with traditional psychological defenses (denial, rationalization, undoing, splitting, projection, and projective identification). Employees are not only anxious about their work and each other, they feel even more anxious because of the consultation and the prospects of change. The result is often a rich mixture of psychologically defensive responses (which are especially important to follow up with questions that probe behind the resistance to talk about events and feelings) and black and white, we versus them descriptions of problems and grievances. It is also critical to pay special attention to the mention of metaphors, stories, myths, heroic deeds, fantasies, and dreams, all of which include unconscious content and associations. These are ways of communicating painful and threatening content about organizational life that cannot be spoken of directly. Appreciating these aspects of communication permits the consultant to develop an in-depth understanding of the psychologically defensive character of the executives and employees interviewed, and the psychologically defensive workplace.

However, the role of the consultant involves more than developing empathy for the executives and employees interviewed and insight into the dysfunctions and psychologically defensive patterns of individual and organizational functioning. The development of a diagnostic impression and accompanying hypotheses about individual and organizational functioning is also facilitated by an appreciation of the intersubjective (projective and transferential) aspects of the workplace, including those related to the consultant, that makes the subjective experience of the workplace what it is (Diamond 1993; Hirschhorn 1988; Stein 1994). Underlying themes of unconscious organizational identity must be located and brought to consciousness for inspection. One rich area for exploration and learning involves projections and transferences onto the consultant by organization members and projections and transferences onto the organization and its members by the consultant. Much can be learned about the unconscious side of the organization by spotting and interpreting bi-directional projective and transferential content.

In sum, the nature of an organization's unconscious identity is revealed by acts of management conveyed as examples, stories, myths, and metaphors during the interviews; such acts as management intimidation, scapegoating, over control, micromanagement, suppression of feelings, promotion of interpersonal and intergroup rivalry and conflict, and avoidance of dealing with profound organizational problems and dysfunctional psychologically defensive leadership styles. These data are supplemented by the experience of the consultant as he or she relates to the organization and its members.

The interviewing process begins the process of metaphorically "prying the lid off" of the repressed or suppressed side of organizational life that no one can safely talk about or often even think about. The "bad stuff" leaks out in every story and metaphor and unaccountable interaction with the consultant, as everyone intuitively knows this knowledge is dangerous and to be feared. As a result, the consultant's role of containing and processing the anxiety and "bad stuff" and outbreaks of suppressing it to "put it back in the box" (to contain it) is often taxed to the limit. These powerful organizational dynamics make the consultant anxious and subject to the emergence of projection and transference on his or her part, as well as psychologically defensive tendencies and practices. During the interviews, the consultant must pay close attention to his or her own levels of anxiety, the level of anxiety present in his or her clients, and their system of intersubjectively developed roles and self, other, and organizational experience; these now include the consultant as a part of the process.

The psychoanalytically informed consultant must, therefore, be prepared to serve as a good enough container for many of these unconscious dynamics (not all, as the client must assume responsibility for some of them from the start in order to promote a pattern of assumption of personal responsibility) so that they can be safely reflected back to the client organization's leadership for discussion and to be worked through. This requires considerable personal wherewithal on the part of the consultant. Confronting resistances to hearing, understanding, and developmental change opportunities, which must be acknowledged to exist in order for them to be overcome by the leadership group, is stressful work.

This work of confronting the resistances often takes the form of testing the validity of the factual findings and intersubjective data uncovered by the interviewing process; the consultant's interpretation of his or her own experiences and feelings, as well as individual, group, and organizational psychologically defensive practices. This requires the consultant to publicly test his or her operative assumptions and hypotheses with the client's leadership group. In particular the consultant must share information about the general themes of privately held employee assumptions about superiors, subordinates, and how the organization seems to really be working. This sensitive and often undiscussable feedback reflects the underlying intersubjective quality of organizational life, which not only contains many productive elements, but also some that are irrational and psychologically defensive in nature. A negotiated reality must emerge between the consultant, leader, and leadership group that forms a basis from which to proceed with the intervention. It is important that the consultant not expect that all of his or her pearls of wisdom and insights will be accepted as valid by the leadership group. However, the consultant must be prepared to advocate for a readily rejected point of view to test whether the group is resistant to the insight or merely rejecting it for reasons that they can explain. It is within this overall context of organizational inquiry, diagnosis, and learning that the model of the psychologically defensive workplace informs the work.

The Psychologically Defensive Appeal to Mastery

Consultants can expect to find that mastery and its accompanying psychologically defensive practices (perfection, arrogance and vindictiveness, and narcissism) are common in the workplace and are especially likely to be found among executives, managers, and supervisors. The identifiable behaviors that accompany these leadership styles are described in Chapter 8. However, another way to look at the appeal to mastery is its effects upon the organization as a whole. A CEO, owner, executive, or manager who is preoccupied with getting control, achieving perfection to avoid criticism, taking on anyone, any time, who is critical of him or her or gets in the way, espousing great ideas with little follow through, and being admired or, failing that, being feared will produce predictably dysfunctional organizational dynamics. These dynamics, if found during the interviewing process, should lead the consultant to believe that the executives involved are engrossed in the psychologically defensive pursuit of mastery.

The nature of the organizational culture and its accompanying shared intersubjective identity will, in the case of mastery, usually be dominated by an executive who relies upon mastery to control his or her anxiety. If it is the CEO, the entire organization is likely to be affected. If an executive further down in the organization is involved, it is likely all the areas under his or her direction will be affected. An organization may have one or more subcultures of mastery.

Employees who feel angry, bitter, and disillusioned about how they are being treated and how the organization is being run will appreciate the opportunity to ventilate their dangerous, anger-filled, and, therefore, often undiscussable feelings. They may report instances of passive resistance or openly fighting back that resulted in victories over management. Others may not be distressed, and describe in glowing terms how their leaders are in control of everything and how much they admire their work (the appeal to love). Some may also not report much interest in how the organization is run or how they are treated (the appeal to freedom). They present themselves as disengaged from their work, accepting or perhaps merely tolerating their place of work, its culture, and its leaders, warts and all. These two responses are discussed in the following sections.

In the case of the appeal to mastery, the interview data will reveal many mastery-oriented organizational attributes. Employees will describe their leader and the workplace as controlling, manipulative, hypercritical, coercive, unpredictable, explosive, managed by intimidation, devious, political (who you know), preoccupied with appearances, containing in groups and out groups, divisive, combative, excessively competitive, out to make him or her (the leader) look good, uncaring, using people, unrewarding, disregarding employee ideas, not open to being questioned, not learning from experience, and punishing, to list but some of the more common employees descriptions of their work experience when an organization's identity is dominated by the psychological appeal to mastery.

Consultants who are repeatedly confronted with such stories, descriptions, and complaints about how employees are treated must conclude that the executive over the area is anxious and reaches out to control everything and everyone, which causes him or her to end up dominating employees and killing off risk-taking innovation and the incentive to cooperate and perform good work. This executive, if asked, may report that he or she is doing a great job and that the organization or the department is doing just fine despite some complaints here and there which are to be expected. This executive, while relying upon psychological defenses such as denial, rationalization, and selective attention or inattention to block out negative information regarding his or her leadership style, may also simply be out of touch with the effects of his or her behavior upon employees. They avoid saying anything out of fear of being punished. The executive simply does not understand the adverse effects of his or her psychologically defensive practices upon the organization.

Should this be the case (it should be tested during the diagnostic phase with the executive), the consultant will be faced with a major challenge during the intervention. The consultant may also inappropriately come to unconsciously identify with the employees who are set upon by the executive. The consultant may come to unwittingly feel that it is his or her job to do something about the executive, such as having him or her disciplined, removed, or retrained, to save the employees. This transference-fed rescue fantasy, while important to acknowledge as valid, must not be permitted to influence the consultant's actions. Similarly, it is possible for the consultant to identify with the "powerful" executive who is signing his or her checks. In this case, the employees will be seen as misunderstanding the executive and contributing to their own suffering by not being team players and good employees who follow direction. Once again, these important projective and transferential thoughts and feelings cannot be ignored, but must also not be acted upon. In both of these cases, transferential data and fantasy should be used to inform the intervention.

The Psychologically Defensive Appeal to Love

Consultants will also have occasion to confront executives and organizational culture and identity that contains many care-giving, self-sacrificial, and interpersonally sensitive qualities. In this case, the organization may have a high social focus (as compared with the high task, win-or-lose dynamics of the appeal to mastery) that compromises task performance. Leaders who rely upon this psychologically defensive practice, as described in Chapter 8, espouse and practice devoted and caretaking behavior toward employees and promote a culture where employees are valued. This leader, however, does not provide clear direction, make effective task assignments, actively direct work, or evaluate employee performance. As a result, the consultant will find a few key employees who have assumed a great deal of informal authority to keep the organization running, make decisions when necessary, and try to hold employees accountable for their performance. This outcome is not all bad and provides those willing to step forward with leadership opportunities. However, these leaders implicitly understand that their boss will not be there to back them up if they run into major problems. They may be left to, metaphorically speaking, "twist in the wind" by their paralyzed leader, a paradoxical outcome given the leader's espoused values.

The culture and organizational identity that is described to the consultant has a soft, even "mushy" quality to it that is frequently infused with a "touchy feely" concern for how employees feel and relate to each other. It is mushy in the sense that there is no decisive and authoritative leadership from the top when appropriate, and the organizational structure is vague. Some employees and even entire areas will be found to be working out of role as a result of gradually assuming ever-greater amounts of responsibility without acquiring matching levels of formal authorization to make decisions and acquire and allocate organizational resources. Stories, myths, and descriptions of organizational life will focus on a few people taking care of or defending everyone and everything. Executives who rely upon this psychologically defensive practice may occasionally be described as doing small caretaking chores for their employees, perhaps several levels down in the organization from themselves. Organizational discipline is frequently lacking (as may occur with the narcissistic practice), and an accumulation of organizational deadwood and "driftwood" (people who constantly move about within the organization) may have developed. Efforts on the part of the consultant to locate examples in which executives and, in some instances, employees have been held accountable, project and work assignments are made consistent with the organizational structure, and employees have clear position descriptions that they adhere to are hard to find. The consultant may also find that one section of the organization has acquired power and influence disproportionate to its mission, creating organizational imbalance. Longevity and who you know may seem to be the keys to advancement. The organization may also be described as a good place to work because it takes care of its people. The organization or division may also have a long history of mediocre performance, but not always, as those who do end up in positions of responsibility may be highly effective despite limited investment with formal authority and recognition. These are all aspects of the organization that will be learned from executive and employee interviews which, if consistently encountered, can be understood to be a description of a psychologically defensive workplace.

The consultant may be seduced into feeling that this culture is the "right way to be." The consultant may also be encouraged to feel valued and cared for by the CEO and executive group and employees. In return, the expectation is that the consultant will also be caretaking, which implies protecting everyone from knowledge that their psychologically defensive organization contains dysfunction. The CEO and leadership group may deny, split off, and project their caretaking attributes onto the consultant, coming to experience themselves as not being able to take care of others and themselves and becoming dependent upon the consultant to fulfill a caretaking role. The consultant will be encouraged to act out this role and to incorporate the projections (projective identification), thereby experiencing him- or herself as a caretaking person who must place a high value on protecting everyone's feelings, something that is inconsistent with being an effective consultant. Once again, intersubjective experience such as this must be acknowledged by the consultant to exist, but must not be acted upon. They are, however, important data that may be used to inform the consultation process.

The Psychologically Defensive Appeal to Freedom

Consultants are less likely to be confronted with an organization that has a culture and unconscious organizational identity that is freedom based, although there are entire nations that have sought it, such as Albania and North Korea. Some organizations prefer to be left alone to function in what sometimes becomes a timeless altered reality without consequences. This may be true of small businesses, or farmers who value rugged individualism. Religious cults and separatist groups espouse the values of being left alone so that they can fulfill their own internally generated laws, rules, and social norms. It is more likely that consultants will find organizational subcultures that are engrossed in pursuing freedom from what are felt to be coercive influences of their parent organization and its management hierarchy. The subcultures will usually have a leader and a number of staff who value their autonomy even when it is counterproductive for the organization.

These freedom- and autonomy-oriented cultures and subcultures espouse values and an operating philosophy of going it alone with a few outstanding (or rugged) individuals who possess the right stuff achieving greatness alone by sheer persistence. Those involved in the culture will speak of the organization as a whole in negative, invasive, coercive, and even paranoid terms, often making it clear that they function better if just left alone. Many of the images, stories, metaphors, and myths discovered during the interviewing process will belabor the values of individual worth, freedom to do what one wants, and the coercive and many times negative effects that the larger organization has upon the subgroup's ability to accomplish work. Intersubjective experience will contain many feelings and images about not being limited or maligned by the organization, being left alone to do their work, and that they are a tight-knit, unique or elite group that does not like outsiders.

Consultants who encounter these organizational dynamics may also have the subculture explained as not being part of the organization, being uncooperative, and not working in support of the larger organizational mission. A we versus them quality will exist to the interviews that focuses on the powerful and hard-to-control separatist leader and the "evil" organization from which uninformed decisions and changes flow. These dynamics are seductive for the consultant and encourage him or her to identify with one side of the organizational split. Feelings on the part of the consultant of wanting to bring the subculture and its leader under control or that the organization is not that good and the subculture has it right should be attended to as pertinent to how powerful these organizational dynamics are. These organizational dynamics also present consultants with a challenging intervention that must be driven by thorough, careful, and unbiased data collection supported by many concrete examples from both sides. Healing the schism or split first requires acknowledging its presence and then developing some sense of mutual understanding and respect.

INTERVENTION IN THE SUPPORT OF ORGANIZATIONAL CHANGE

Psychoanalytically informed interventions imply being able to systematically and forcefully, but also sensitively and carefully confront leaders, executives, employees, and groups about the dysfunctional nature of their psychologically defensive workplace. The consultant must lead the chief executive, leadership group, and employees in a process of acknowledging their psychologically defensive thoughts, feelings, and actions and how they influence their working together, the structural design of their organization, and how assigned roles are enacted by employees. This work enables organization members to begin to change their thoughts and feelings about themselves, each other, work, and the organization in order to overcome the dysfunctional aspects of their psychologically defensive workplace and achieve better individual, group, and organizational performance. Accomplishing this requires the development of interpersonal trust and a sense that it is safe to do the work of confrontation and resolution, which requires open examination of heretofore unquestionable aspects of work life.

The Development of a Safe Holding Environment

Leaders, their close associates who constitute the leadership group, their subordinates, and even the employees of the organization must find it safe to work together to discuss the psychologically defensive workplace. Participants in the intervention process must reflect, analyze, confront, predict, invent, innovate, and recreate themselves, their groups, and their organization's structure and culture in a safe, trusting, and supportive setting. Accomplishing these tasks requires a context in which it is safe to share negative feelings and often uncomfortable feedback from the organizational diagnosis, including acknowledging that some errors in judgement may have occurred. In particular, the past must be explored for the origins of current problems stemming from the psychologically defensive workplace. Everyone participating must be able to join together in open debate about mapping a new future for their organization and how this new vision will be fulfilled. The presence of psychologically defensive practices must be spotted and open to discussion in order to avoid their disrupting the work of recreation. Interpersonal trust must be nurtured to new levels, as putting aside one's familiar and dependable psychologically defensive practices is no easy matter. Interpersonal vulnerability emerges, which enables self-reflective personal and organizational growth and development. This is especially important for the leader, who is often felt to be unapproachable and cannot be challenged without grave threat to one's well-being. This sensitive work with the leader may, in part, fall to the consultant.

In psychodynamic terms, the holding environment created for the leadership group with the support of the consultant must be able to contain anxiety that promotes the use of psychological defenses and the psychologically defensive practices. In particular, projections of aggression and destructive fantasies, some of which are aimed at the consultant for bringing out all of the "bad or dangerous stuff" for discussion, must be contained and reflected back by the consultant to encourage reflective group process. This work, however, may well be thought or more accurately, felt to be too dangerous and better just left alone (resistance to change). It must also be acknowledged that the consultant, by becoming a container for many of the denied, split-off, and projected feelings of aggression, is readily located as the source of all of the negative thoughts and feelings, and therefore the obvious person to scapegoat. The role of container is challenging for consultants, who are strongly encouraged to incorporate the projected aggression, thereby not only making them aggressive in the eyes of those in the leadership group, but also experienced as such by themselves. However, it is critical that the consultant not accept the projections, tacitly support his or her scapegoating, or promote dependency. He or she must share this experience with the leadership group so as to encourage ownership or reintegration of the projections and promote the assumption of personal responsibility for the disowned thoughts, feelings, and attributes that accompany the need for change. The ability to serve as a container, while simultaneously directing the work of the leadership group and organization members in discovering new ways of thinking, feeling, and acting, requires that the consultant have a systematic and well-understood theoretical perspective from which to promote the challenging and often personally fragmenting work of organizational change. Once again, the model of the psychologically defensive workplace is of assistance.

The Psychologically Defensive Appeal to Mastery

Leading an effective intervention that addresses leadership styles and organizational dynamics that possess deeply embedded, mastery-oriented psychological practices is challenging. Open discussion sponsored by the consultant may be received as threatening and promote paranoid and persecutory anxiety that leads to a greater reliance upon the appeal to mastery. When this occurs, everyone and everything has to be controlled, including everyone's thoughts and feelings and the "bad" consultant. The consultant may be criticized as imperfect, insensitive, unrealistic, and not understanding. He or she may be openly aggressed by senior management, including being threatened with termination. A process of one-upmanship may ensue among the executives in the leadership group, as each tries to best contribute to the change process, or some may become envious of the consultant who appears to be receiving much sought after respect and admiration. These dynamics will exist in some form or another and their presence will ebb and flow with the anxiety being felt within the leader, leadership group, and employees.

When more than one consultant is involved, these dynamics are often acted out in ways that tend to split the consultants apart. One may be labeled as "bad" and the other as "good," and, given time, these labels may change back and forth between the consultants, promoting even greater personal and interpersonal fragmentation. When splitting is present, the consultants incorporate the projections and experience themselves as falling apart in their ability to work together, which in many ways mirrors the interior life of the leadership group and its members. Locating these splits, reflecting upon them, and healing them when they occur within the consulting pair or group is essential for learning more about the psychologically defensive workplace and remaining effective contributors to the creative and reflective process of organizational change. These considerations apply equally well to the appeals to love and freedom.

Intervention efforts to minimize or remove the dysfunctional aspects of mastery are focused on the frequent and unquestioned (or unquestionable) resort to power and control that occurs on the part of the CEO, leadership group, managers, or supervisors, depending upon how far down in the organization it occurs or perhaps where in the organization it occurs if a subculture is involved. The consultant reflects back to the leadership group what has been found in the interviews to support this mastery interpretation of their leadership and organizational dynamics. Concrete examples are provided; however, the names of those who provided the examples are omitted. The omission is usually easy, because the examples are frequently common knowledge within the organization and are often cited by many who are interviewed. In the event the CEO or owner is the focal point of the mastery problem (which may well be the case), one-on-one discussion and coaching should take place before work commences in an open setting with members of the leadership group and employees. The CEO must learn about the negative effects that his or her style has upon the organization. The appeal to mastery may essentially be the character of the CEO and, in such a case, organizational and leadership change amounts to trying to work with a character disorder (Kets de Vries 1991). Exceptional care and sensitivity is required on the part of the consultant to be able to discuss the CEO's leadership style without becoming overly threatening and thereby provoking too much anxiety. At the same time, the consultant must avoid the temptation to view this work as psychotherapy, which it is not. If the CEO is ultimately unwilling to face the issues that his or her mastery-oriented leadership style raise for the organization, the consultation and intervention may end at this point. If the CEO is willing to concede that there are problems and acknowledge a willingness to work on them, then the larger organizational intervention may begin. However, this only occurs if the CEO is willing to openly discuss his or her leadership style with the consultant and, eventually, the leadership group, and expresses a willingness to try something new. These same considerations apply equally to other executives, with the exception that resistance may be overcome by the CEO if the consultant is not able to overcome it in a voluntary, timely, and meaningful way.

The actual process of organizational intervention involves developing an understanding of the psychologically defensive appeal to mastery and how it affects employees and operations. Once again supported by concrete examples, the leadership group is led through a process of reenvisioning the kinds of leadership styles that will best serve their organization. The concept of an intentional leadership style is discussed, and longitudinal advice, counseling, and coaching are provided by the consultant to enable the executives to make the change and avoid backsliding to the old familiar psychologically defensive ways.

Managers, supervisors, and employees must also be informed of what is understood to be the current mastery-oriented organizational culture and identity, including its drawbacks in terms of achieving better performance. Once there is general agreement as to what the organization's culture and identity are, a new vision must be developed and presented by the leadership group (not the consultant). Employees may be provided with different forms of participation, information, and training to support unlearning the old ways and creating and learning the new ones.

The Psychologically Defensive Appeal to Love

This appeal presents consultants a much different challenge than that of mastery. In this case, the CEO, leadership group, managers, and supervisors must, while retaining their humanist orientation, add a task orientation to their work which makes it acceptable to set clear and challenging goals, with timelines, and hold employees accountable for accomplishing them.

If the data show that the appeal begins with the CEO, the same proviso as with the appeal to mastery applies. One-on-one discussion and coaching is desirable. The CEO must be encouraged to feel that it is not only acceptable but desirable to provide firm direction and hold his or her staff accountable for meeting mandated or agreed-to goals. It is important to appreciate that this CEO may possess many codependent personality qualities, and in order to make the consultant happy and receive his or her approval and support the CEO may agree to make a change in his or her leadership style and even act it out as long as the consultant is present. Should this occur, backsliding will follow as a result of these behaviors being for the most part foreign to the CEO, who only embraces them to please the consultant. It is, therefore, important to be able to work with the CEO over a long period, sometimes spanning years, to enable him or her to learn that the new behavior is adaptive and that it does not lead to negative outcomes for him- or herself.

A deeply entrenched appeal to love will exist if many in the leadership group have been selected or converted to the underlying values of being dependent and caretaking. In this case, the consultant must provide the group with feedback and concrete examples of where this approach has created problems (vague job descriptions, accumulation of deadwood, lack of clear direction and coordination of work), and, if possible, documentation of poor performance. The consultant must bring forward issues such as clarifying organizational structure and position descriptions, and developing a well-documented strategic plan with accompanying goals and measurable objectives. A review of staffing levels and dysfunctional employees is also likely to be in order. All of these actions will make the leadership group anxious, as they implicitly conflict with the focus on taking care of (protecting) everyone's feelings. The consultant must, however, persist by showing that not doing this part of the work is compromising organizational success, something no one will want to claim as a goal.

The Psychologically Defensive Appeal to Freedom

In general, this is not likely to be an adaptive choice of defense for an entire organization, although there are exceptions. Consultants are more likely to find it within organizations where divisions and departments develop their own subcultures, some of which may be based upon the appeal to freedom. The intervention is also likely to be supported by the CEO and the leadership team (even if some members are acting out the appeal to freedom). Consultation diagnostic feedback to the CEO and leadership group will include examples of how the excessive pursuit of autonomy, combative avoidance-oriented intraorganizational interactions, poor interpersonal communication and self-regulation, and the development of a subset of goals that are inconsistent with achieving the organization's mission are compromising organizational performance. Providing examples that show where financial losses and losses of market share have occurred are especially productive in getting the CEO's and leadership group's attention. Efforts to scapegoat the individuals, divisions, and departments involved are to be avoided. It must be acknowledged that the development of and maintenance of these dysfunctional subcultures with their own deviant organizational identities is, in part, the responsibility of the CEO and leadership group for letting it happen in the first place. It should also be noted that when scapegoating occurs it fulfills the subgroup's fantasy that the organization is bad and needs to be avoided.

Intervention into areas diagnosed as preoccupied with autonomy and espousing a we versus them attitude toward the larger organization must be approached with care, in that external intervention will be felt to be a coercive, unwanted influence that should be avoided. After all, if the area was right before, nothing has changed just because a consultant is working with the leadership group. Care must be taken to meet with the subculture's leader or leadership group in a low-key, non-threatening manner in which learning is emphasized. Every effort should be made to avoid making them anxious. However, the consultant must sustain a constant press for learning and change, and should work with employees by providing participation, communication, and training formats as appropriate.

The Mixed Intervention

Large, complex organizations are likely to have many divisions, many layers of management, and even multiple CEOs. The result is a rich organizational stew that contains many types of psychologically defensive cultures and organizational identities. This occurs even in small organizations, although it is more common to locate one predominate or dominating psychologically defensive practice within them. The big organization presents the consultant with a challenge, not only in gathering interviewing data (it may involve hundreds of interviews) but also in understanding the interrelationships of the various unconscious interpersonal and intraorganizational agendas.

Intervention must start with the CEO if he or she sets the tone for psychologically defensive organizational dynamics. If not, then working with the CEO to understand the dysfunctional psychologically defensive aspects of his or her organization will provide both the CEO and the consultant with a rich learning opportunity. In this case, the consultant collaborates with the CEO and his or her leadership group to design a series of coordinated interventions to facilitate change. Also to be considered are such things as how rational the entire organization's structure is. Many organizations grow organically, without much thought to organizational efficiency and effectiveness, and often in ways that avoid creating conflict or resolving it. Restructuring and role clarification may become the overarching recommendations which, when combined with strategic planning and work redesign, provide an organization with a comprehensive plan for renewal (Diamond and Allcorn 1986).

In sum, large organizations are the ultimate challenge for the psychoanalytically informed consultant. Effectiveness will be in large part determined by the CEO's interest and personal investment in the consultation.

SUMMARY

This chapter explains how the model of the psychologically defensive workplace helps to organize the consultation process. The model provides an understandable and readily applied comprehensive and systematic perspective for organizing data collection during the organizational diagnostic phase, and informs efforts to promote organizational change in a direction of greater intentionality.

THE PSYCHOLOGICALLY DEFENSIVE WORKPLACE **10**

Its Implications for Organizations, Research, and Daily Living

> In all organizations, trust and open communication in groups are required if we are to look critically at ourselves and our work and thereby further our efforts. Yet throughout modern organizational life, such trust and dialogue are often lacking. Listening to everyone, not engaging in frenetic activity to flee from listening, is the heart of group morale, task performance, and productivity, I try to tell myself. Yet that early ideal has somehow been eclipsed by the compulsion toward action, the illusion of total control, and the pursuit of profit.
>
> Stein 1994, 136

> The psychoanalytic perspective on organizations offers workers possibilities for competence by revealing a more accurate, richer organizational map. In shedding light on unconscious meanings of bureaucratic relationships, this perspective helps workers identify aspects of organizations to which they normally respond unconsciously. By opening these meanings to examination, this orientation helps workers recognize more of what influences them, including some of their normally tacit assumptions and reject others as self-defeating. They may then more realistically assess and deploy resources available to them.
>
> Baum 1987, 167

This book has explored the psychologically defensive workplace. Along the way, the dysfunctional, darker, unconscious and irrational side of organizational life has been illuminated by the model of the psychologically defensive workplace. The model provides a psychoanalytically informed context for understanding the thoughts, feelings, and actions of employees, managers, and chief executives working under stressful conditions. It also explains the more difficult aspects of understanding interpersonal relationships and group and organizational dynamics. Underscored throughout the book is the realization that the emergence of the psychologically defensive workplace during stressful times threatens organizational vitality and long-term survival.

All organizations, subcultures, and interpersonal relations contain irrational and psychologically defensive elements. These defenses exist to a lesser extent in organizations that have a culture that minimizes uncertainty about oneself, others, and the organization. However, along a curve that is bell shaped, there are organizations that are less able to allay employee anxiety; some even promote it. The predictable response of executives and employees to potentially avoidable internal organizational stresses and unavoidable external stresses is reliance upon psychological defenses and the character-like psychologically defensive practices. This book has explained the nature of, effects of, and possible avoidance or resolution of these unconscious, psychologically defensive influences, with an eye to making executives and employees more reflective and intentional. There are, however, a few more issues to be discussed.

This chapter concludes the book by examining the implications of the model of the psychologically defensive workplace for managing people, work, and organizations in the future. Equally important issues are how this book informs subsequent research and theory building related to managing the psychologically defensive workplace, and the implications of the psychoanalytically informed model for managing our daily lives outside of work which, the reader is reminded, exist in an interactive whole with the workplace.

MANAGING PEOPLE, WORK, AND ORGANIZATIONS IN THE FUTURE

This book has made clear how complex organizational life really is and how strange it may become when work life becomes filled with stress. CEOs, executives, managers, supervisors, and employees are all, at times, confronted with stressful situations that create excessive amounts of anxiety and reliance upon familiar psychological defenses to cope with the anxiety and stressors. The question raised throughout this book has not been if it happens, but what happens when it does. How does one respond to regain more intentional and self-reflective managerial and employee thoughts, feelings, and actions?

The problem is that there are no easy, one-through-ten quick-fix steps to dealing with the issues raised by the presence of the psychologically defensive workplace. Learning to effectively manage to avoid the development of excessive anxiety and to better contain it and its negative effects in the event it does occur, however, is not a hopeless aspiration. Being effective translates into first understanding and appreciating the psychologically defensive workplace in order to be able to avoid and change it. This understanding must be translated into active learning and new expectations for leaders and followers.

Learning to Manage the Psychologically Defensive Workplace

The essence of being more effective is demanding and suggests that leaders, executives, and employees strive to work beyond themselves in order to gain the personal development needed to achieve intentionality and sustain reflectivity during stressful times. Accomplishing this implies the development of new forms of continuing education and staff development focused at understanding the psychologically defensive workplace and psychologically defensive employee proclivities that adversely affect others and work.

One way to accomplish this is by using an integrated reading, lecture, and experiential learning methodology. Participants learn in the classroom about the psychologically defensive workplace, while also having a chance to experience and explore it in an experiential setting, outside of work, in which participants, as a group, are confronted with a stressful situation (a teaching methodology pioneered by the authors). The experiential learning opportunity teaches, firsthand, how the participants, others, and the group respond to stress and accompanying anxiety. This integrated learning approach produces new learning, reflective self-insights, and a much greater appreciation of the unconscious and psychologically defensive side of group and organizational dynamics. It is perhaps the best and most direct way to learn about oneself and the psychodynamic aspects of the psychologically defensive workplace.

Another learning method involves establishing a corporate learning environment or culture where organizational dynamics, including the actions of others, are open to inspection and discussion. The openness and, more importantly, interpersonal trust and respect that must be present in order for this learning strategy to blossom are, however, often lacking and, if present, may be pushed to their limits in the process of establishing the open, learning environment. Once again, even though critical incidents often provoke the emergence of anxiety and the psychologically defensive workplace, careful nurturing of an open, learning, and, therefore, resilient organizational culture may be assisted by the use of external consultants trained in the work of overcoming the psychologically defensive workplace (Allcorn 1991; Diamond 1993).

Demands on Leaders

The model of the psychologically defensive workplace emphasizes the powerful influence leaders have upon employees (and vice versa). Leaders work under a lot of pressure that is generated from both external expectations placed upon them and internal expectations that they may never meet. CEOs, executives, managers, or anyone in a leadership role should pay attention to workplace pressures as well as feelings of being anxious when difficult and sometimes out-of-control relationships and events occur.

Becoming reflective is not a hopeless task and, in fact, it is a task that must be undertaken in order to become more effective. Leaders must pay attention to what is going on around them and how they are feeling in response. This takes commitment and practice to accomplish. Being able to recognize and label events as stressful is a first step. Being able to actively sense and label one's feelings of anxiety as well as other emotions—fear, anger, humiliation, envy, frustration, and desire, to list but a few important workplace emotions—is an equally important step (Allcorn 1991). Once they are labeled, which implies acknowledging and thinking about events and feelings, an opportunity is created to reflect upon this awareness and its anxiety-ridden nature, as well as one's psychologically defensive tendencies to respond to stress. Then, one can select a more intentional behavior that is grounded in the workplace.

Accomplishing these steps takes practice. Experiencing a resistant and combative employee response to a request can lead to immediately feeling irritated, if not angry, which may then result in acting upon the anger and escalating the dysfunction of the moment. However, being able to label the response as resistant and combative in one's mind encourages reflection upon the nature of the response, including consideration of the employee's possible underlying motivations. At the same time, being aware of rising feelings of irritation and anger (labeling them as such) may also be reflected upon as reasonable feelings given the provocation, but it is important to avoid acting upon them (Allcorn 1994). Accomplishing this internal work permits the executive involved to ponder why the employee has responded in such a way, while, at the same time, not acting upon feelings of irritation and anger. Reflecting back to the employee his or her apparent resistance to taking instruction creates an opportunity to communicate and better understand the employee's response, which may be motivated by factors completely unrelated to the executive, the instruction, or even the workplace.

In sum, becoming a reflective and intentional leader translates into being able to understand and think through what is happening, including having an appreciation of one's own thoughts and feelings before responding.

Demands on Followers

The model of the psychologically defensive workplace makes clear that followers not only frequently engage in the psychologically defensive practices but are very likely going to expend considerable unconsciously motivated effort trying to control executives and colleagues. This workplace behavior, while natural, is potentially filled with dysfunction when the workplace and working relationships with executives become stressful, thereby provoking psychologically defensive responses.

Followers, like their leaders, have a responsibility to be aware of what is going on around them that makes them anxious and provokes emotions such as fear and anger. They must also be able to understand their feelings and manage them without resorting to the psychologically defensive practices and related psychological defenses. In particular, employees must be able to understand the anxiety-ridden aspects of the presence of power and authority held by executives. Being able to accept one's role as follower is critically important in terms of improving individual and organizational performance (Kelly 1988). These requirements of an effective follower are met in much the same way as leaders must meet them, which in many ways demonstrates that behind workplace titles and roles lies a human condition that is shared in common by everyone in the workplace. Developing the ability to be self-reflective and intentional is equally important for followers.

Implications of the Psychologically Defensive Workplace for Organizational Culture and Identity

The model of the psychologically defensive workplace presents CEOs, executives, teachers, and consultants with a challenge. The workplace must become more effective by minimizing avoidable stress and anxiety, and it must also be transformed to enable employees to effectively manager their anxieties when stress is not avoidable. These considerations lead to the need to develop a more open, communicative, collaborative, and supportive workplace, in which what is going on and how it is being experienced is open to discussion and, therefore, change. Executives and employees must be encouraged to join together in accomplishing this demanding aspect of managing the psychologically defensive workplace. These considerations translate into envisioning a form of organizational culture that promotes a less psychologically defensive organizational identity in which anxiety does not need to be managed through denial, splitting, projection, and projective identification.

The elements that compose this less psychologically defensive organizational identity and workplace culture have been explained throughout this book. The reader is again reminded that organizational performance is compromised in many different ways by the emergence of the psychologically defensive workplace. What is being suggested here is not a people-first, humanist point of view that is disconnected from the harsh realities of the workplace and making a profit. Rather, the workplace can become more effective, dynamic, and creative if the presence of the psychologically defensive practices are minimized and reflectivity and intentionality are enhanced. This, however, implies acknowledging the unconscious motivations of many executive and employee thoughts, feelings, and actions that are the basis for the psychologically defensive workplace. Finding new, creative, organization-specific ways to address this demanding new vision holds considerable promise for improved organizational performance as we approach the twenty-first century.

THE CHALLENGE FOR ORGANIZATIONAL RESEARCH
AND THEORY BUILDING IN THE FUTURE

Understanding the psychologically defensive side of the workplace is criti-cal to managing its downside. Effectively managing the psychologically defen-sive aspects of the workplace begins with a conceptual model for understanding it. This book provides the psychologically defensive workplace model that encourages it to be challenged by the development of alternative models and empirical evaluation of its veracity.

Challenging the Model of the
Psychologically Defensive Workplace

The model of the psychologically defensive workplace is but one way to approach building a comprehensive model for understanding the uncon-scious, intersubjective aspects of the workplace and their influence upon or-ganizational dynamics and performance. In particular, Karen Horney's theories, it may be asserted, are out of date, although throughout the book many connections have been made to contemporary theoretical perspectives such as object relations theory and self-psychology.

Additional Theory Building

Theory building is important intellectual work. The development of theo-ries forms the basis for empirical research, as is illustrated by the continuing research that tests Einstein's theory of relativity. Theory building and, in par-ticular, the development of comprehensive models that provide a systematic approach to understanding intrapersonal, interpersonal, group, and organiza-tional dynamics are challenging, as there are few psychoanalytic theoretical perspectives of sufficient depth and breadth to be expanded to encompass the psychologically defensive workplace.

Most of what has been written on psychoanalytic theory provides the reader a rich milieu in which to think about one's unconscious motivations. How-ever, most of the development of theory is scattered and lacks the develop-ment of overarching theories that tie together the ideas of those who continue to research and think and write about the applications of psychoanalytic theory to understanding human development and functioning.

The challenge posed to those interested in developing more complete, sys-tematic, and comprehensive theories of the workplace is to be able to incorpo-rate a psychoanalytically informed perspective that promotes understanding intrapersonal, interpersonal, group, and organization dynamics as well as the relationship of the workplace to society. Each of these levels of analysis must be explicated and interconnected to create a multidimensional perspective of the workplace that avoids reliance upon a dialectical grab bag of different theoretical perspectives and interpretations that the executive or consultant intuitively fits to the situation. Intuitive processes such as these are all to often fed by their own unconscious processes, such as projection and transference that contaminate data collection, interpretation, and intervention. Avoiding these outcomes is the purpose of relying upon a comprehensive and systematic theoretical perspective.

Empirical Testing

The theoretical model described in this book is sufficiently systematic and operationalized to permit the inquiring minds of empiricists to attempt to test it (Roemer 1986). Testing the model, however, requires the use of research methods that permit locating and measuring unconscious psychologically defensive content. This is no small challenge, as unconscious process itself is extraordinarily hard to quantify. Methods that have been used to test the model and others like it include California Q-sort, Q-methodology, and other, more labor-intensive methods of testing that rely upon projective instruments such as the Rorschach and TAT (thematic apperception testing) in which stories are developed from pictures.

Testing psychoanalytically based models raises the hermeneutical challenge of how to study subjectivity (Brown 1980). As much as possible, testing must avoid imposing the researcher's point of view upon his or her research subjects, something that occurs in the development of hypotheses and the imposition of rigid and preestablished testing instruments such as Q-sort cards. Empirical testing of unconscious psychologically defensive processes is a challenge that is yet to be adequately met by empirical scientists (Edelson 1984).

BEYOND THE WORKPLACE: USING THE THEORY OF THE PSYCHOLOGICALLY DEFENSIVE WORKPLACE TO INFORM DAILY LIVING

The skeptic (which we all need to be) will question whether the model of the psychologically defensive workplace informs one's daily life. A healthy degree of skepticism, especially regarding psychoanalytically informed theory building (and its reductionistic tendencies), is important and presses those who develop theory to make it applicable to daily life. It is our assertion that the model of the psychologically defensive workplace presented in this book not only informs the management of organizational life, it also informs the living of one's life outside of the workplace. The following slice-of-life vignette is provided to illustrate how the psychoanalytically informed theory of the workplace is helpful in understanding our lives outside of work.

Tom was dressed and ready to go to work; all he needed was breakfast. His wife June, however, was slow this morning in preparing breakfast for him and Sally, their fifteen-year-old daughter who was having a bad hair day. No matter how June worked with Sally, she insisted that she just wanted to be left alone (the appeal to freedom) to get ready for school. However, she did not appear to be making fast-enough progress to get her fed and out of the house on time to catch the school bus. June became insistent and demanded that she come to the kitchen for breakfast otherwise she would be grounded the rest of the week (the appeal to mastery—arrogant–vindictive, win or lose). This led to more resistance from Sally, which made June feel ignored, frustrated, and angry. When Sally finally arrived in the kitchen, she slammed her books down and handled her food and breakfast dishes harshly (displaced anger and aggression). Tom decided to leave to avoid June, who was now clearly infuriated with Sally (the appeal to freedom).

On his way to work, he found himself stranded at a train crossing with a slow-moving train. After a few minutes he could feel his anger beginning to boil. Why should this happen to him today? What did he do to deserve such treatment? He was really feeling that the rules for social behavior and, in fact, reality should not apply to him, as he was a very special person (the appeal to mastery—arrogance and narcissism). As his anger mounted, he could do little but wait helplessly for the train to pass.

Upon arriving at work late his boss greeted him with a major problem that had arisen during the night shift. By now Tom was really in no mood to deal with it and his response was, "Why me?" (the appeal to freedom). He went on to point out that he was not particularly qualified to deal with it, that others were available who could deal with the problem, and that it would be better if someone else dealt with it (the appeal to love—dependency upon others to take charge).

His boss, however, saw it differently and made it absolutely clear that Tom was going to deal with the problem—or else (the appeal to mastery—arrogant–vindictive, win or lose). This further increased Tom's anger and anxiety. Tom's response was that he had other important work and he wanted to be left alone to do it (the appeal to freedom).

This slice-of-life vignette need be taken no further. In the time it took Tom to get out of bed and to work, there occurred a number of instances where the model of the psychologically defensive workplace informs understanding Tom's daily life, those with whom he relates, and the interconnection of the workplace with the rest of one's life. Tom, having had a bad morning getting to work, was, to his boss, inexplicably resistant to doing the work being requested.

SUMMARY

This book is devoted to developing a more complete understanding of the psychologically defensive workplace, which all too often gets in the way of working together to achieve organizational success. A great deal has been explained and explored regarding the implications of psychologically defensive behavior for leaders, followers, educators, and organizational consultants. Yet much more could be said to better explain the many nuances of the model. The model, in fact, offers a basis for interpreting and understanding the vast complexity of the workplace and many possible case applications can be described and discussed. However, what is perhaps more important to appreciate is that the model of the psychologically defensive workplace offers those desiring to understand organizational dynamics a conceptual vantage point from which to look out upon the vast panorama of organizational dynamics that exists on a daily basis and takes on new dimensions during stressful times. The model of the psychologically defensive workplace is above all else, a way of systematically thinking about organizational life and how it may be managed to improve individual and organizational performance.

APPENDIX

This appendix is a matrix that explains the interactions of five psychological defenses with the psychologically defensive practices. The matrix illustrates the often paradoxical nature of psychologically defensive responses to anxiety. For example, in the case of the perfectionist, the wish to achieve perfection and avoid painful knowledge of imperfection goes unknown (a compromise formation). Paradoxically, this individual, who strives for perfection and seeks to avoid painful knowledge that threatens an idealized self-image of perfection, minimizes opportunities to improve his or her performance. The wish to view one's self-image as perfect takes precedence over learning and achieving excellence. The possibility of imperfection (such as the human tendency to make errors) does not exist as a possibility in the mind of the perfectionist. If criticized, the perfectionist may respond in a childlike fashion, with hurt feelings, by discounting the person offering the criticism, or by striking back with criticism. As a result, rather than encouraging others to report errors that improve performance, the perfectionist discourages feedback to maintain an idealized self-image of perfection. This makes achieving excellence unlikely.

This process is supported by the splitting of the self into two parts, one perfect and one imperfect. The concomitant projection of the imperfect part onto others serves to protect the perfectionist from threats to his or her idealized perfect self-image. Imperfection and inferiority are attributed to others, which artificially inflates the perfectionist's self-esteem by comparison.

This appendix illustrates these same kinds of paradoxical outcomes for the remaining defensive practices. Developing an appreciation of the complex relationships presented here prepares the reader to appreciate the book. Each psychologically defensive practice (perfectionist, arrogant–vindictive, narcissistic, self-effacing, and resigned) is briefly discussed relative to five common psychological defenses (repression, regression, splitting, projection, and projective identification).

PERFECTIONIST

Repression

Feeling unworthy of respect and admiration because of imperfect performance and personal attributes and associated feelings of self-contempt are removed from consciousness in favor of knowing oneself to be perfect and, therefore, worthy of respect and admiration, permitting identification with a perfect idealized self-image.

Regression

Interpersonal events that create feelings of being deficient and imperfect are responded to with over-determined needs to achieve perfection and/or find fault with others by being openly contemptuous of them and hypercritical of their performance or personal attributes.

Splitting

Ideal perfect self-images and despised imperfect self-images are split apart. The bad images are denied to exist in preparation for their projection onto others, thereby leaving perfection and the likelihood of not being criticized.

Projection

Bad imperfect aspects of self are projected onto others who are then found to be imperfect. This permits them to be denigrated and criticized as needed to maintain the desired idealized self-image of being better (more perfect) than others.

Projective Identification

As an innocent child, parental projections of imperfection and self-contempt are accepted. The child then understands he or she is imperfect and contemptible and not deserving parental approval. The child responds to this undesirable self-knowledge and feeling of rejection by trying to more perfectly meet parental expectations which are seldom met. Unqualified approval, therefore, escapes the child.

ARROGANT–VINDICTIVE

Repression

Feeling helpless, dominated, not respected, worthless, and associated feelings of low self-confidence and self-respect, fear, and rage are disposed of from consciousness in favor of knowing oneself to be powerful and fearless enough to defeat others, thereby permitting identification with a powerful, admired, and proud idealized self-image.

Regression

Interpersonal events that create feelings of being humiliated, beaten, and subordinated by malevolent others are responded to with over-determined needs to fight back and dominate others. This may include childlike rages and temper tantrums.

Splitting

Bad parts associated with feelings of being helpless, not respected and worthless are split off, denied to exist, and projected onto others, thereby leaving self-feelings of being powerful and worthy of respect and admiration.

Projection

Helpless, malevolent, devious, and worthless parts of self are projected onto others, who are then known (with nearly absolute certainty) to not deserve to be respected. They are also believed to be blocking and frustrating this individual's pride-filled pursuits and ambitions, thereby meriting attack and defeat.

Projective Identification

Parental projections of being helpless, defeated, and dominated by malevolent others are accepted by the child as part of him- or herself. As a result, the child feels helpless and dominated by his or her parents, who tend to over-control the child for his or her own good. The child resists the domination by fighting back to acquire and maintain self-pride.

NARCISSISM

Repression

Knowledge of having been made to feel unworthy of admiration and respect and associated feelings of self-hate and contempt for others who have withheld approval and love are removed from consciousness in favor of knowing oneself to be an outstanding performer who has few flaws. This individual feels that he or she deserves to be admired, thereby permitting identification with an idealized, grandiose self-image that includes having the big ideas, being a benefactor or savior of others, and being someone with few self-doubts.

Regression

Interpersonal events that arouse feelings of not being admired are responded to with anger and overdetermined efforts to manipulate others into being admiring, or by possibly abandoning the situation in a burst of rage in favor of locating understanding others who will admire what one has to offer.

Splitting

Good self-images of being admired and bad self-images of being unworthy of admiration are split apart, with the intent of retaining the good self-images and emptying oneself of the bad self-images. These undesirable self-images are attributed to others who do not then deserve to be admired and who, therefore, need to be taken care of in return for their loyal respect and admiration.

Projection

Bad self-images of being unworthy of admiration are projected onto others, who are then understood to be unworthwhile and in need of being cared for. However, they are also expected to provide this benevolent individual with grateful admiration, which reinforces the ideal self-image of being worthwhile and in charge.

Projective Identification

Parental projections of not being admirable are accepted by the child, who then understands he or she is not admired and, therefore, must be taken care of by benevolent parents who deserve to be admired in return. The child, however, resists these feelings by working hard to merit admiration from others. Later, as an adult who works hard to portray an image worthy of being admired, this individual strives to control the thoughts and feelings of others to insure respect and admiration.

SELF-EFFACING

Repression

Anger and rage, feeling despised and unworthy of love and approval by parental figures, are repressed from consciousness in favor of maintaining a self-image that is not threatening or offensive and, therefore, worthy of love and being taken care of. Passive resignation and self-knowledge of being helpless and in need of being protected emerge. Caretaking others are served without regard to sacrifices of personal pride and integrity, in order to maintain love and dependency and continued identification with the lovable ideal self-image.

Regression

Interpersonal events that arouse feelings of being unfit, unlikable, abandoned, or mistreated are responded to with over-determined needs to find love and safety. Actions may include crying, acting helpless, and selflessly serving the needs of others in return for their loving and caring.

Splitting

Bad unlovable parts associated with being effective, fighting back, and being in control are split off for projection onto others thereby leaving images of being powerless, dependent, and lovable. This individual is willing to make any sacrifice to gain the love and caretaking attention of powerful others.

Projection

Bad self-images of being powerful, effective, and in control are projected onto others, who are understood to be worthwhile, and effective and who it is expected will love and take care of this individual in return for selfless love, all of which reinforces the despised self-image of being helpless and needy.

Projective Identification

Parental projections of despised feelings of being dominant and powerful are accepted by the child, who then understands he or she is despised for these tendencies and, therefore, must not act out these tendencies to receive parental love and caretaking. Later, as an adult who abhors feeling powerful and in control, this individual encourages others to act powerfully.

RESIGNED

Repression

Knowledge of having been dominated and controlled by parental figures and being unable to cope with ever-present interpersonal conflict and associated feelings of self-hate, fear, and contempt are disposed of from consciousness. This disposal permits identification with an idealized self-image that is free of stressful, conflicting, and coercive interpersonal relationships and personal aspirations. Change and coping with conflict are avoided to sustain this self-image.

Regression

Interpersonal events that arouse feelings of being needed or dominated by others are responded to with over-determined needs to avoid others and their coercive influences. Freedom from conflict and anxiety is sought, which may include angry sulking, isolation, and abrupt withdrawal from interactions.

Splitting

Bad aspects of self associated with being powerful, controlling, able to act, caretaking, helpless, passive, or dependent are split off and denied in anticipation of projection onto others, thereby leaving images of being free of these tendencies and at peace with oneself.

Projection

Bad self-images are projected onto others who are understood to be either powerful and controlling or helpless and seeking dependence, both of which are to be avoided if conflict-free peace of mind is to be maintained.

Projective Identification

Parental projections of paranoid fears and anxieties of being unable to regulate interactions with others who are understood to be either seeking to dominate and control or assuming roles of dependency are accepted by the child, who then understands that he or she should be suspicious of others (parents are experienced as controlling and desiring love). The child responds by trying to avoid entangling relationships with his or her parents and others.

REFERENCES

Allcorn, Seth. *Anger in the Workplace*. Westport, Conn.: Quorum, 1994.

Allcorn, Seth. *Codependency in the Workplace*. Westport, Conn.: Quorum, 1992.

Allcorn, Seth. "Keep Individuality in Top Management." *Personnel* 69 (4):17–22 (1990).

Allcorn, Seth. "Leadership Styles: The Psychological Picture." *Personnel* 65 (4):46–54 (1988).

Allcorn, Seth. "The Self-Protective Actions of Managers." *Supervisory Management* 34 (1):3–7 (1989a).

Allcorn, Seth. *Working Together*. Chicago: Probus, 1995.

Allcorn, Seth. *Workplace Superstars in Resistant Organizations*. New York: Quorum, 1991.

Allcorn, Seth. "Understanding Groups at Work." *Personnel* 66 (8):28–36 (1989b).

Allcorn, Seth, Howell Baum, Michael Diamond, and Howard Stein. *The Human Cost of a Management Failure: Organizational Downsizing at General Hospital*. Westport, Conn.: Quorum, 1996.

Argyris, Chris. *Personality and Organization*. New York: Harper and Row, 1957.

Argyris, Chris, and Donald Schon. *Organizational Learning: A Theory of Action Perspective*. Reading, Mass.: Addison-Wesley, 1978.

Argyris, Chris, and Donald Schon. *Theory in Practice: Increasing Professional Effectiveness*. San Francisco: Jossey-Bass, 1974.

Astin, Alexander, and Rita Scherrei. *Maximizing Leadership Effectiveness*. San Francisco: Jossey-Bass, 1980.

Bar-Levav, Reuven. *Thinking in the Shadow of Feelings*. New York: Simon and Schuster, 1988.

Barnard, Chester. *Organization and Management*. Cambridge: Harvard University Press, 1948.

Basset, Glenn. *Management Styles in Transition*. New York: American Management Association, 1966.

Baum, Howell. *The Invisible Bureaucracy*. New York: Oxford University Press, 1987.

Baum, Howell. *Organizational Membership*. Albany: State University of New York Press, 1990.

Bennis, Warren. *Why Leaders Can't Lead*. San Francisco: Jossey-Bass, 1989.

Bierce, Ambrose. *The Devil's Dictionary*. New York: Dover, 1958.

Bion, Wilfred. *Experiences in Groups*. London: Tavistock, 1961.

Block, Dorothy. *So the Witch Won't Eat Me: Fantasy and the Child's Fear of Infanticide*. Boston: Houghton Mifflin, 1978.

Block, Peter. *Flawless Consulting*. San Diego: Pfeiffer and Company, 1981.

Bowlby, John. *Attachment and Loss*. New York: Basic Books, 1969.

Bowlby, John. *Loss: Sadness and Depression*. New York: Basic Books, 1980.

Bowlby, John. *Separation Anxiety and Anger*. New York: Basic Books, 1973.

Brown, Steven. *Political Subjectivity*. New Haven, Conn.: Yale University Press, 1980.

Crozier, Michel. *The Bureaucratic Phenomenon*. Chicago: University of Chicago Press, 1964.

Czander, William. *The Psychodynamics of Work and Organizations*. New York: Guilford Press, 1993.

Denhardt, Robert. *In the Shadow of Organization*. Lawrence: University of Kansas Press, 1981.

Deutsch, Helene. *Neurosis and Character Types*. New York: International Universities Press, 1965.

Diamond, Michael. "Bureaucracy as Externalized Self-System." *Administration and Society* 16 (2):195–214 (1984).

Diamond, Michael. "The Social Character of Bureaucracy: Anxiety and Ritualistic Defense." *Political Psychology* 6 (4):663–679 (1985).

Diamond, Michael. "Treating the Parataxic Organization: A Case Example of Organizational Meaning." *Administration and Society* 23 (4):61–80 (1991).

Diamond, Michael. *The Unconscious Life of Organizations*. New York: Quorum, 1993.

Diamond, Michael, and Seth Allcorn. "The Psychodynamics of Regression in Work Groups." *Human Relations* 40 (8):525–543 (1987).

Diamond, Michael, and Seth Allcorn. "Psychological Barriers to Personal Responsibility." *Organizational Dynamics* 12 (4):66–77 (1984).

Diamond, Michael, and Seth Allcorn. "Psychological Responses to Stress in Complex Organizations." *Administration and Society* 17 (2):217–239 (1985).

Diamond, Michael, and Seth Allcorn. "Role Formation as Defensive Activity in Bureaucratic Organizations." *Political Psychology* 7 (4):709–732 (1986).

Downs, Anthony. *Inside Bureaucracy*. Boston: Little, Brown, and Co., 1967.

Edelson, Marshall. *Hypothesis and Evidence in Psychoanalysis*. Chicago: University of Chicago Press, 1984.

Euripides. "Orestes." In *The Complete Greek Tragedies*, translated by William Arrowsmith. Chicago: University of Chicago Press, 1958.

Fairbairn, William. *Psychoanalytic Studies of Personality*. London: Tavistock, 1952.

Fenichel, Otto. *Collected Papers of Otto Fenichel*. Edited by H. Fenichel and D. Rapaport. New York: Norton, 1954.

Freud, Sigmund. *A General Introduction to Psychoanalytic Theory*. Paris: Payot, 1921.

Freud, Sigmund. *Group Psychology and the Analysis of the Ego*. New York: Norton, 1922.

Freud, Sigmund. "Repression." In *The Freud Reader,* edited by P. Gay. 1915. Reprint, New York: Norton, 1989.

Getzels, Jacob, and Egon Guba. "Social Behavior and the Administrative Process." *School Review* 65 (Winter) 423–441 (1957).

Grotstein, James. *Splitting and Projective Identification*. Northvale, N.J.: Jason Aronson, 1985.

Guntrip, Harry. *Schizoid Phenomena, Object Relations and the Self*. New York: International Universities Press, 1969.

Hirschhorn, Larry. *The Workplace Within*. Cambridge: MIT Press, 1988.

Hodgson, Richard, Daniel Levinson, and Abraham Zaleznik. *The Executive Role Constellation*. Cambridge: Harvard University Press, 1965.

Horney, Karen. *Neurosis and Human Growth*. New York: Norton, 1950.

Hummel, Ralph. *The Bureaucratic Experience*. New York: St. Martin's Press, 1977.

Jacoby, Henry. *The Bureaucratization of the World*. Berkeley and Los Angeles: University of California Press, 1973.

Jaques, Elliot. "Social Systems as a Defense Against Persecutory and Depressive Anxiety." In *New Directions in Psychoanalysis*, Edited by M. Klein, P. Heimann, and R. E. Money-Kryle. New York: Basic Books, 1955.

Kelly, Robert. "In Praise of Followers." *Harvard Business Review* 66 (6):142–148 (1988).

Kernberg, Otto. *Borderline Conditions and Pathological Narcissism*. New York: Jason Aronson, 1975.

Kernberg, Otto. *Internal World and External Reality*. Northvale, N.J.: Jason Aronson, 1980.

Kernberg, Otto. "Regression in Organizational Leadership." *Psychiatry* 42: 24–39 (1979).

Kets de Vries, Manfred. "Managers Can Drive Their Subordinates Mad." *Harvard Business Review* 57 (4):125–134 (1979).

Kets de Vries, Manfred, ed. *The Irrational Executive*. New York: International Universities Press, 1984.

Kets de Vries, Manfred, and Danny Miller. *The Neurotic Organization*. San Francisco: Jossey-Bass, 1984.

Kets de Vries, Manfred, and Sidney Perzow, eds. *Handbook of Character Studies*. Madison, Conn.: International University Press, 1991.

Kilmann, Ralph, and Ines Kilmann. *Manager Ego Energy*. San Francisco: Jossey-Bass, 1994.

Klein, George. *Psychoanalytic Theory*. New York: International Universities Press, 1976.

Klein, Melanie. *Contributions to Psycho-Analysis, 1921–1945*. London: Hogarth Press, 1948.

Knezevich, Stephen. *Administration of Public Education*. New York: Harper and Row, 1969.

Kohut, Heinz. *The Analysis of the Self: A Systematic Approach to the Psychoanalytic Treatment of Narcissistic Personality Disorders*. New York: International Universities Press, 1971.

Kohut, Heinz. *How Does Analysis Cure?* Chicago: University of Chicago Press, 1984.

Kohut, Heinz. *The Restoration of the Self*. New York: International Universities Press, 1977.

Kraus, William. *Collaboration in Organizations: Alternatives to Hierarchy*. New York: Human Sciences Press, 1980.

LaBier, Douglas. *Modern Madness*. New York: Touchstone Books, 1986.

Laplanche, Jean, and Jean Pontalis. *The Language of Psychoanalysis*. New York: W.W. Norton, 1973.

Lasch, Christopher. *The Culture of Narcissism*. New York: W.W. Norton, 1979.

Lasch, Christopher. *The Minimal Self*. New York: W.W. Norton, 1984.

Levinson, Harry. *Executive*. Cambridge: Harvard University Press, 1981.

Levinson, Harry. *Organizational Diagnosis*. Cambridge: Harvard University Press, 1972.

Levinson, Harry. *Psychological Man*. Cambridge: The Levinson Institute, 1976.

Lippitt, Gordon. *Organizational Renewal*. Englewood Cliffs, N.J.: Prentice-Hall, 1969.

Maccoby, Michael. *The Gamesman*. New York: Basic Books, 1976.

Mahler, Margaret, Fred Pine, and Anni Bergman. *The Psychological Birth of the Human Infant*. New York: Basic Books, 1975.

Masterson, James. *The Search for the Real Self*. New York: The Free Press, 1988.

May, Rollo. *The Meaning of Anxiety*. New York: Washington Square Press, 1977.

Menzies, Isabel. "A Case in the Functioning of Social Systems as a Defense against Anxiety: A Report of a Study on the Nursing Service of a General Hospital." *Human Relations* 13 :95–121 (1960).

Menzies, Isabel. *The Functioning of Social Systems as a Defense against Anxiety*. London: Tavistock, 1970.

Modell, Arnold. *Psychoanalysis in a New Context*. Cambridge: Harvard University Press, 1984.

Morgan, Gareth. *Images of Organization*. Newbury Park, Calif.: Sage, 1986.

Ogden, Thomas. *The Matrix of the Mind*. Northvale, N.J.: Jason Aronson, 1990.

Reddin, William. *Managerial Effectiveness*. New York: McGraw-Hill, 1970.

Roemer, Walter. "Leary's Circle Matrix: A Comprehensive Model for the Statistical Measurement of Horney's Clinical Concepts." *The American Journal of Psychoanalysis* 46 (3):249–261 (1986).

Rycroft, Charles. *A Critical Dictionary of Psychoanalysis*. Totowa, N.J.: Littlefield, Adams, and Co., 1968.

Sandler, Joseph, ed. *Projection, Identification, Projective Identification*. New York: International Universities Press, 1987.

Schafer, Roy. *A New Language for Psychoanalysis*. New Haven, Conn.: Yale University Press, 1976.

Schein, Edgar. "Organizational Culture." *American Psychologist* 45 (2):109–119 (1990).

Schein, Edgar. *Organizational Culture and Leadership*. San Francisco: Jossey-Bass, 1985

Schon, Donald. *The Reflective Practitioner*. New York: Basic Books, 1983.

Schwartz, Howard. *Narcissistic Process and Corporate Decay*. New York: New York University Press, 1990.

Shapiro, Edward, and Wesley Carr. *Lost in Familiar Places*. New Haven, Conn.: Yale University Press, 1991.

Sperling, Otto. "Psychoanalytic Aspects of Bureaucracy." *Psychoanalytic Quarterly* 19:88–100 (1950).

Srivasta, Suresh, and Associates. *The Executive Mind*. San Francisco: Jossey-Bass, 1983.

Stein, Howard. *Listening Deeply*. Boulder, Colo.: Westview Press, 1994.

Stein, Howard. "Social Role and Unconscious Complementarity." *Journal of Psychoanalytic Anthropology* 9 (3):235–268 (1986).

Stern, Donald. *The Interpersonal World of the Infant*. New York: Basic Books, 1985.

Sullivan, Harry. *The Interpersonal Theory of Psychiatry*. New York: Norton, 1953.

Tansey, Michael, and Walter Burke. *Understanding Counter-Transference*. Hillsdale, N.J.: The Analytic Press, 1989.

Terry, George, and Roger Hermanson. *Principles of Management*. Homewood, Ill.: Learning Systems, 1970.

Turquet, Pierre. "Threats to Identity in the Large Group." In *The Large Group: Therapy and Dynamics*. edited by L. Kreeger. Itasca, Ill.: Peacock, 1975.

Weber, Max. *The Theory of Social and Economic Organization*. New York: The Free Press, 1947.

Winnicott, Donald. *The Maturation Processes and the Facilitating Environment*. New York: International Universities Press, 1965.

Zaleznik, Abraham. *Human Dilemmas of Leadership*. New York: Harper and Row, 1966.

Zaleznik, Abraham, and Manfred Kets de Vries. *Power and the Corporate Mind*. 2d Ed. Chicago: Bonus Books, 1985.

INDEX

ABOUT THE AUTHORS

SETH ALLCORN is a principal of DyAd, a consulting firm in Asheville, North Carolina. For twenty years he was an academic health-science center executive, during which time he wrote seven other books, more than fifty papers, and contributed several chapters to various volumes edited by others.

MICHAEL A. DIAMOND is Professor of Public Administration at the University of Missouri–Columbia, where he teaches and writes on the psychodynamics of organizational change. He is a principal of DyAd, and a past president of the International Society for the Psychoanalytic Study of Organizations. Dr. Diamond received the American Psychological Association's 1994 Harry Levenson Award for Excellence in Consulting Psychology. Among his various publications is *The Unconscious Life of Organizations* (Quorum, 1993).